First World War
and Army of Occupation
War Diary
France, Belgium and Germany

33 DIVISION
Divisional Troops
Divisional Trench Mortar Batteries
29 May 1916 - 31 January 1919

WO95/2413/7

The Naval & Military Press Ltd
www.nmarchive.com
Published in association with The National Archives

Published by

The Naval & Military Press Ltd

Unit 10 Ridgewood Industrial Park,

Uckfield, East Sussex,

TN22 5QE England

Tel: +44 (0) 1825 749494

www.naval-military-press.com

www.nmarchive.com

This diary has been reprinted in facsimile from the original. Any imperfections are inevitably reproduced and the quality may fall short of modern type and cartographic standards.

© Crown Copyright
Images reproduced by permission of The National Archives, London, England, 2015.

Contents

Document type	Place/Title	Date From	Date To
Heading	WO95/2413/7		
Heading	33rd Division Divl Artillery Divl Trench Mortar Btts. Oct 1915-Feb 1919		
War Diary	Becordel Near Fricourt	31/08/1916	31/08/1916
War Diary	Vendin-Lez-Bethune	29/05/1916	29/05/1916
War Diary	Vendin	01/06/1916	01/06/1916
War Diary	Annequin	02/06/1916	02/06/1916
War Diary	Vendin	10/06/1916	18/06/1916
War Diary	Annequin	20/06/1916	07/07/1916
War Diary	Fricourt	24/07/1916	24/07/1916
War Diary	Becordel	13/08/1916	31/08/1916
Heading	War Diary For August 1916 Of X 33 T.M Battery Vol		
War Diary		01/08/1916	27/08/1916
War Diary		01/08/1916	31/08/1916
War Diary	Becordel Becourt	01/09/1916	05/09/1916
War Diary	Bonnay	06/09/1916	06/09/1916
War Diary	Naours	07/09/1916	07/09/1916
War Diary	Boisbergues	08/09/1916	08/09/1916
War Diary	Le Marais Sec	09/09/1916	09/09/1916
War Diary	Lattre-St-Quentin	10/09/1916	15/09/1916
War Diary	Humbercamps	16/09/1916	16/09/1916
War Diary	Ligny-St-Flochel	17/09/1916	28/09/1916
War Diary	Souastre	29/09/1916	30/09/1916
Heading	War Diary X 33 T.M. Battery September 1916		
Miscellaneous			
War Diary	Becordel	01/09/1916	10/09/1916
War Diary	Lattre St Quentin	10/09/1916	29/09/1916
War Diary	Beendel	01/09/1916	05/09/1916
War Diary	Bonnay	06/09/1916	06/09/1916
War Diary	Naours	07/09/1916	07/09/1916
War Diary	Boisbergues	08/09/1916	08/09/1916
War Diary	Milly	09/09/1916	09/09/1916
War Diary	Lattre St. Quentine	10/09/1916	14/09/1916
War Diary	Souastre	15/09/1916	30/09/1916
War Diary	Becordel	01/09/1916	30/09/1916
War Diary	Souastre	01/10/1916	10/10/1916
War Diary	Bayencourt	11/10/1916	31/10/1916
War Diary	Souastre	01/10/1916	01/10/1916
War Diary	Hebuterne	01/10/1916	01/10/1916
War Diary	Bayencourt	11/10/1916	17/11/1916
War Diary	Talmas	22/11/1916	22/11/1916
War Diary	Bailleul	23/11/1916	25/11/1916
War Diary	Dreuil Le Hamel	26/11/1916	30/11/1916
War Diary		01/11/1916	26/11/1916
War Diary	Bayencourt	01/11/1916	22/11/1916
War Diary	Talmas	22/11/1916	23/11/1916
War Diary	Bailleul	23/11/1916	26/11/1916
War Diary	Dreuil-Le Hamel	26/11/1916	30/11/1916
Heading	Hdqrs 33rd Div		
War Diary		01/11/1916	30/11/1916

War Diary	Dreuil Le Hamel		01/12/1916	10/12/1916
War Diary	Camp No 13		11/12/1916	11/12/1916
War Diary	Bray-Sur-Somme		12/12/1916	15/12/1916
War Diary	No 14 Camp		16/12/1916	16/12/1916
War Diary	Bray-Sur-Somme		17/12/1916	26/12/1916
War Diary	Vaux En-Amienois		27/12/1916	31/12/1916
War Diary	Le Hamel		02/12/1916	31/12/1916
War Diary	Dreuil Le Hamel		01/12/1916	01/12/1916
War Diary			01/12/1916	31/12/1916
War Diary			02/12/1916	31/12/1916
War Diary	Vaux-En-Amienois		01/01/1917	04/01/1917
War Diary	Longpre-Les-Corps-Saints		05/01/1917	31/01/1917
War Diary	Le Hamel		01/01/1917	04/01/1917
War Diary	Longpre		05/01/1917	07/01/1917
War Diary	Vaux		07/01/1917	17/01/1917
War Diary	Longpre		18/01/1917	25/01/1917
War Diary	Frise		25/01/1917	31/01/1917
War Diary	Dreuil		01/01/1917	04/01/1917
War Diary	Longpre		05/01/1917	25/01/1917
War Diary	Frise		25/01/1917	28/01/1917
War Diary	Trenches		29/01/1917	31/01/1917
War Diary			01/01/1917	31/01/1917
War Diary	Longpres-Les-Corps-Saints		01/02/1917	04/02/1917
War Diary	Frise		05/02/1917	28/02/1917
War Diary	Frise		01/02/1917	28/02/1917
War Diary	Trenches		01/02/1917	28/02/1917
War Diary	Frise Bend		01/02/1917	28/02/1917
War Diary	Frise		01/03/1917	11/03/1917
War Diary	Sailly-Le Sec		11/03/1917	25/03/1917
War Diary	Naours		26/03/1917	27/03/1917
War Diary	Mezzerolles		28/03/1917	28/03/1917
War Diary	Bouret-Sur-Conche		29/03/1917	29/03/1917
War Diary	Arras		30/03/1917	31/03/1917
War Diary	Frise		01/03/1917	11/03/1917
War Diary	Sailly-Le-Sec		12/03/1917	25/03/1917
War Diary	Naours		26/03/1917	26/03/1917
War Diary	Mesexalles		27/03/1917	27/03/1917
War Diary	Bourt-Sur-Canche		28/03/1917	28/03/1917
War Diary	Arras		31/03/1917	31/03/1917
War Diary	Frieze		01/03/1917	30/03/1917
War Diary	Arras		31/03/1917	31/03/1917
War Diary	D17A 55-30 Sheet 28 NEI		01/03/1917	01/03/1917
War Diary	D17C 40-80 Sheet 28 NEI		31/03/1917	31/03/1917
War Diary	Clary Sector		01/03/1917	08/03/1917
War Diary	Frise Bend		09/03/1917	10/03/1917
War Diary	Sailly Le Sec		11/03/1917	24/03/1917
War Diary	Naours		25/03/1917	26/03/1917
War Diary	Mezerolles		27/03/1917	27/03/1917
War Diary	Bouret S/Canche		28/03/1917	28/03/1917
War Diary	Arras		29/03/1917	01/04/1917
War Diary	Blangy		02/04/1917	10/04/1917
War Diary	Arras		11/04/1917	21/06/1917
War Diary	Boiry St Martin		22/06/1917	30/06/1917
War Diary	Arras		01/06/1917	21/06/1917
War Diary	Boiry St Martin		22/06/1917	30/06/1917
War Diary	Arras		01/06/1917	21/06/1917

War Diary	Boiry St Martin	22/06/1917	30/06/1917
War Diary	Arras	01/06/1917	20/06/1917
War Diary	Boiry St Martin	21/06/1917	25/07/1917
War Diary	Coxyde Bains	26/07/1917	31/07/1917
War Diary	Boiry St Martin	01/07/1917	24/07/1917
War Diary	Doullens	25/07/1917	26/07/1917
War Diary	Coxyde Des Bains	27/07/1917	31/07/1917
War Diary	Boiry St Martin	01/07/1917	26/07/1917
War Diary	Boiry St Martin	01/07/1917	22/07/1917
War Diary	Doullens	23/07/1917	24/07/1917
War Diary	Coxyde Belgium	25/07/1917	31/07/1917
War Diary	Coxyde Bains	01/08/1917	31/08/1917
War Diary	Coxyde Bains	01/08/1917	05/09/1917
War Diary	Hallebast Corner	06/09/1917	30/09/1917
War Diary	Coxyde Bains	01/09/1917	03/09/1917
War Diary	Hardinfort	04/09/1917	06/09/1917
War Diary	Hallebast Corner	17/09/1917	30/09/1917
War Diary	Coxyde Bains	01/09/1917	04/09/1917
War Diary	Hardifort	06/09/1917	06/09/1917
War Diary	Hallebast Corner	06/09/1917	30/09/1917
War Diary	Coxyde Bains	01/09/1917	02/09/1917
War Diary	Hardifort	03/09/1917	04/09/1917
War Diary	Hallebast Corner	05/09/1917	01/10/1917
War Diary	Dickebusch	02/10/1917	21/10/1917
War Diary	Hallebast Corner (Dickbusch)	22/10/1917	31/10/1917
War Diary	Hallebast Corner	01/10/1917	31/10/1917
War Diary	Hallebast (Corner)	01/10/1917	31/10/1917
War Diary	Hallebast Corner	01/10/1917	30/11/1917
War Diary	Hallebast Corner	01/11/1917	04/11/1917
War Diary	Le Nieppe	05/11/1917	12/11/1917
War Diary	Bouvelinghem	13/11/1917	30/11/1917
War Diary	Hallebast Corner	01/11/1917	30/11/1917
War Diary	Hallebast Corner	01/11/1917	03/11/1917
War Diary	Le Nieppe	04/11/1917	11/11/1917
War Diary	Bouvelinghem	12/11/1917	30/11/1917
War Diary	Bouvelinghem	01/12/1917	02/12/1917
War Diary	Hardifort	03/12/1917	03/12/1917
War Diary	Vlamertinghe	04/12/1917	04/12/1917
War Diary	Potijze	05/12/1917	31/12/1917
War Diary	Bouvelinghem	01/12/1917	31/12/1917
War Diary	Bouvelinghem	01/12/1917	01/12/1917
War Diary	Hardifort	02/12/1917	02/12/1917
War Diary	Vlamertinghe	03/12/1917	03/12/1917
War Diary	Potijze	04/12/1917	31/12/1917
Heading	A.D.A. & Q.M.G. War Diary (Original) For January herewith		
War Diary	Potijze	01/01/1918	28/01/1918
War Diary	Vlamertinghe	29/01/1918	29/01/1918
War Diary	Ouve Wirquin	30/01/1918	31/01/1918
War Diary	Vaux-En-Amienois	01/01/1918	05/01/1918
War Diary	Potijze	06/01/1918	29/01/1918
War Diary	Ouve-Wirquin	30/01/1918	31/01/1918
War Diary	Ouve Wirquin	30/01/1918	21/02/1918
War Diary	Potijze	22/02/1918	28/02/1918
War Diary	Ouve-Wirquin	01/02/1918	03/02/1918
War Diary	Vaux-En-Amienois	04/02/1918	19/02/1918

War Diary	Potijze	23/02/1918	31/03/1918
Heading	33rd Divisional Artillery X & Y Trench Mortar Batteries 33rd Division April 1918		
War Diary	Potijze	01/04/1918	13/04/1918
War Diary	Ypres	14/04/1918	14/04/1918
War Diary	Vlamertinghe	15/04/1918	17/04/1918
War Diary	Browne Camp	18/04/1918	28/04/1918
War Diary	Quintin	29/04/1918	29/04/1918
War Diary	Near Nine Elms Camp	30/04/1918	30/04/1918
War Diary	Potijze	01/04/1918	12/04/1918
War Diary	(Ypres)	12/04/1918	12/04/1918
War Diary	Vlamertinghe	13/04/1918	29/04/1918
War Diary	Near Nine Elms Camp Sheet 27 L.10.C.3.2	01/05/1918	13/05/1918
War Diary	Droglandt	14/05/1918	23/05/1918
War Diary	Pontypool Camp	24/05/1918	31/05/1918
War Diary	Sheet 27 L.10 Central	01/05/1918	13/05/1918
War Diary	Winnezeele	14/05/1918	24/05/1918
War Diary	Pontypool Camp	24/05/1918	31/05/1918
War Diary	Pontypool Camp 27 E.17.B.9.7	01/06/1918	05/06/1918
War Diary	28/A 14.Q.3.3	07/06/1918	29/06/1918
War Diary	In The Field	01/06/1918	30/06/1918
War Diary	28/A 14.A.3.3	01/07/1918	31/07/1918
War Diary		01/07/1918	31/07/1918
War Diary	28/A 14.A.3.3	01/08/1918	31/08/1918
War Diary	27/A 14.A.3.3	01/08/1918	31/08/1918
War Diary	Proven	01/09/1918	01/09/1918
War Diary	Canettemont	02/09/1918	15/09/1918
War Diary	Le Transloy	16/09/1918	20/09/1918
War Diary	Equancourt	21/09/1918	30/09/1918
War Diary		01/09/1918	30/09/1918
War Diary	Peiziere	01/10/1918	08/10/1918
War Diary	Aubencheul	09/10/1918	09/10/1918
War Diary	Malincourt	10/10/1918	10/10/1918
War Diary	Lefayt	12/10/1918	24/10/1918
War Diary	Forest	26/10/1918	31/10/1918
War Diary	Peiziere	01/10/1918	08/10/1918
War Diary	Aubencheul	09/10/1918	09/10/1918
War Diary	Malincourt	10/10/1918	31/10/1918
War Diary	Forest	01/11/1918	04/11/1918
War Diary	Poix Dunord	05/11/1918	06/11/1918
War Diary	Sart Bara	07/11/1918	10/11/1918
War Diary	Berlaimont	11/11/1918	14/11/1918
War Diary	Croix	15/11/1918	15/11/1918
War Diary	Clary	16/11/1918	16/11/1918
War Diary	Les Rues Des Vignes	17/11/1918	30/11/1918
War Diary	Forest	01/11/1918	04/11/1918
War Diary	Poix Du Nord	05/11/1918	06/11/1918
War Diary	Sart Bara	07/11/1918	08/11/1918
War Diary	Berlaimont	14/11/1918	14/11/1918
War Diary	Croix	15/11/1918	15/11/1918
War Diary	Clary	16/11/1918	30/11/1918
War Diary	Walincourt	01/12/1918	07/12/1918
War Diary	Tincourt	08/12/1918	08/12/1918
War Diary	Proyart	09/12/1918	09/12/1918
War Diary	Longeau	10/12/1918	10/12/1918
War Diary	Dreuil Les Molliens	11/12/1918	11/12/1918

War Diary	Villers Campsart	12/12/1918	15/12/1918
War Diary	Inval Boiron	16/12/1918	31/12/1918
War Diary	Walincourt	01/12/1918	07/12/1918
War Diary	Tincourt	08/12/1918	08/12/1918
War Diary	Proyart	09/12/1918	09/12/1918
War Diary	Longeau	10/12/1918	10/12/1918
War Diary	Dreul Les Molliens	11/12/1918	11/12/1918
War Diary	Villers Campsart	12/12/1918	15/12/1918
War Diary	Inval-Boiron	16/12/1918	29/01/1919
War Diary	Inval-Boiron	13/01/1919	29/01/1919
War Diary	Potijze	01/01/1919	27/01/1919
War Diary	Vlamertinghe	27/01/1919	27/01/1919
War Diary	Ouve Wirquin	29/01/1919	31/01/1919
War Diary	Neuville Coppegueule		

WO 91/24136(?)

33RD DIVISION
DIVL ARTILLERY

DIVL TRENCH MORTAR BTTS.
OCT 1916 - FEB 1919

Sheets 1 to 2. Sheet 1

WAR DIARY of V 33 HEAVY TRENCH MORTAR BATTERY.

Army Form C. 2118.

or

~~INTELLIGENCE~~ SUMMARY.

(Erase heading not required.)

Vol I

Instructions regarding War Diaries and Intelligence Summaries are contained in F. S. Regs, Part II. and the Staff Manual respectively. Title pages will be prepared in manuscript.

Place	Date	Hour	Summary of Events and Information	Remarks and references to Appendices
RECORDEL near FRICOURT	3/5/16		Up to the present time a diary for this Unit has not been kept, but the principle events from formation to present time.	
VENDIN-LEZ- BETHUNE	29/5/16		Unit formed Officers:- CAPTAIN J.S. CAMPBELL R.F.A. from 156 Bde R.F.A. A.M.A.N. COLUMN and 2nd LIEUT R.A. JACOBS from 162 B.A.C.; other ranks from 33rd Div. Arty. Details left after re-formation of 33rd D.A.C.	
VENDIN	1/6/16		Battery sent as working party to ANNEQUIN and divided between CUINCHY and AUCHY GROUPS. The N.C.O.s were being distributed among the Field Batteries to assist in Emolacing and repairing gun pits and shelters. 2nd LIEUT. P.C. MANLEY R.F.A. posted from A/162 Bde R.F.A.	
ANNEQUIN	2/6/16			
VENDIN	10/6/16		Battery returned from ANNEQUIN to D.A.C. Camp.	
VENDIN	11/6/16		Battery proceeded to 1st Army School of Trench Mortars for instruction on 240mm Trench Mortar.	
VENDIN	18/6/16		Battery returned from 1st Army School of Mortars	
ANNEQUIN	20/6/16		Battery moved to Trench Mortar billets at P6 & S6 No 9 and were employed as working parties for Field Batteries and Medium Trench Mortar Batteries until 7/7/16	

Sheets 1 to 2   Sheet 2

WAR DIARY of V33 Heavy Trench Mortar Battery
or
INTELLIGENCE SUMMARY.

Army Form C. 2118.

(Erase heading not required.)

Place	Date	Hour	Summary of Events and Information	Remarks and references to Appendices
ANNEQUIN	28/6/16		CAPTAIN J.S. CAMPBELL R.F.A. transferred as D.T.M.O. to Naval Division	
ANNEQUIN	29/6/16		CAPTAIN W.L. POWRIE R.F.A. late O.C. 162 B.A.C. placed in charge vice Capt. J.S. CAMPBELL	
ANNEQUIN	7/7/16		Battery detached to Brigades and D.A.C. for duty and commence to 4th Army Scheme: CAPT W.L. POWRIE to command the S.A.A. section of D.A.C. and 2nd LIEUT R.A. JACOBS to H.Q.S. 162 Bde R.F.A.	
FRICOURT	24/7/16		2nd LIEUT R.A. JACOBS wounded and sent to England	
BÉCORDEL	13/8/16		Battery recalled from Brigades and D.A.C.	
BÉCORDEL	14/8/16		Capt W.L. POWRIE and 25 other ranks proceed to 4th Army School of Mortars for instruction on 9.45 Mortars. The remainder under LIEUT F.C. MANLEY joined a working party for 3rd Medium Trench Mortar Batteries.	
BÉCORDEL	24/8/16		Party returned from 4th Army School of Mortars.	
BÉCORDEL	26/8/16		Lieut F.C. MANLEY proceeded with 2 S.O.R. to 4th Army School of Mortars for instruction. Remainder employed as working parties or on drill.	
BÉCORDEL	31/8/16		So far no guns or equipment have been received by the Battery but we are making progress in drill, physical exercise, signalling etc.	

W.L. Powrie Capt R.F.A.
V 33 H.T.M. Battery

Vol 1

Original

WAR DIARY FOR AUGUST
1916
OF X 33 T.M. BATTERY

Original

Army Form C. 2118.

WAR DIARY
of
INTELLIGENCE SUMMARY.
(Erase heading not required.)

Instructions regarding War Diaries and Intelligence Summaries are contained in F. S. Regs., Part II. and the Staff Manual respectively. Title pages will be prepared in manuscript.

Hour, Date, Place	Summary of Events and Information	Remarks and references to Appendices
August 1-4	Battery employed on 33rd D.A.C. Ammunition Dump at FRICOURT CIRCUS	
" 4.	Returned to bivouac Ahwiff 33rd D.A.C. at BECORDEL.	
" 10	4 reinforcements received from 33rd D.A.C.	
" 12.	Half the battery went into action in HIGH WOOD relieving Z33 TM? and taking over three guns in shell holes. Badly shelled on the night of the 12th, and moved forward into the front line in HIGH	
" 13	WOOD to escape barrage on support trench. No orders for firing received, but ordered not to fire on E. side of WOOD, because of mine. Left HIGH W WOOD on evening of 13th, and returned to BECORDEL.	
" 14 to 16	Constructed emplacements in SEAFORTH TRENCH S10.6.6.4. for two guns.	
" 18	Two detachments went into action with two guns at S10.6.6.4 and fired 39 rounds at S.L.d. 8.0. from 12.15 p.m. – 1.45 p.m. Returned to BECORDEL when finished.	
" 27f	Half the battery assisted in construction of emplacements in HIGH WOOD for the use of Z33 TM Battery.	

H C Powell Lieut
O.C X 33 T M Battery

WAR DIARY or INTELLIGENCE SUMMARY.

Y 33 Trench Mortar Battery

Army Form C. 2118.

Hour, Date, Place	Summary of Events and Information	Remarks and references to Appendices
August 1916:—		
1st to 4th	In bivouac at FRICOURT Ammunition Dump.	
5th to 10th	In bivouac at BECORDEL Ammunition Dump	
1st to 8th	2/Lt T. WINGATE temporarily attached to 150th Brigade R.F.A. You month of August attached to 33rd D.A.C. for discipline. During the month the battery did fatigues for D.A.C. also dug emplacement & tunnels in taking habitat to trench.	
24th August	Went into action in HIGH WOOD fires 80 rounds	
10th to 31st	In bivouac at BECORDEL	

N W Nicholson Lieut
O.C. /33 T M B/y

Z 33 TM Bty Army Form C. 2118.

WAR DIARY
or
INTELLIGENCE SUMMARY

(Erase heading not required.)

Hour, Date, Place	Summary of Events and Information	Remarks and references to Appendices
August 1916		
1st – 4th	In Bivouac at FRICOURT ammunition dump, battery attached 33rd DAC on dump	
5th – 7th	In bivouac at BECORDEL " " " " " "	
8th – 12th	Half of battery in action in HIGH WOOD. One casualty, corporal wounded.	
12th – 31st	In bivouac with 33rd DAC at BECORDEL. Supplied in conjunction with other batteries guides & fatigue parties for making replacements etc.	

E.J. Fitzgerald
Lieut
OC Z 33 Trench Mortar Bty

Sheets 3 to 5 Sheet 3 September

WAR DIARY V/33 Heavy Trench Mortar Battery — Vol 2

Army Form C. 2118.

Place	Date	Hour	Summary of Events and Information	Remarks and references to Appendices
Bécordel–Bécourt	1/9/16		The Battery not being in action the men continued training in Rifle Drill, Foot drill & Physical Drill. Weather — Wet	
Bécordel–Bécourt	2/9/16		Training as above continued. Weather — Wet	
Do	3/9/16		Do — Showery — No 15116 Gnr Taylor C.A. to Hospital	
Do	4/9/16		Do — Wet	
Do	5/9/16		Do — Wet	
BONNAY	6/9/16		Left BÉCORDEL at 7-0 AM and Marched with No 4 Section B.A.C. to BONNAY arriving 12-0 noon. Weather — Showery — Roads bad and muddy	
NAOURS	7/9/16		Left BONNAY at 7-0-50 AM and Marched with No 4 section to NAOURS arriving 6 pm. Weather — Sunny	
BOISBERGUES	8/9/16		Left NAOURS at 10-30 AM marched on before to BOISBERGUES arriving 3-30 pm. Weather — Sunny	
LE MARAIS SEC	9/9/16		Left BOISBERGUES at 1-45 pm. marched as before to LE MARAIS SEC near DOULLENS. Weather — Dull	
LATTRE–ST–QUENTIN	10/9/16		Left LE MARAIS SEC at 7-25 AM. marched to LATTRE-ST-QUENTIN arriving 4 pm. Weather — Dull	
Do	11/9/16		Drill, rifle, foot, Semaphore, Physical. Weather, Showery	
Do	12/9/16		Do. Weather — Dull & Showery	
Do	13/9/16		Do — Dull	
Do	14/9/16		Do — Do.	

Sheets 3 to 5 — Sheet 4 — September

WAR DIARY 1/33 Heavy Trench Mortar Battery

Army Form C. 2118.

INTELLIGENCE SUMMARY.

(Erase heading not required.)

Place	Date	Hour	Summary of Events and Information	Remarks and references to Appendices
LATTRE-ST-QUENTIN	15/9/16		Drill, rifle, foot, semaphore, physical. Weather - Dull	
HUMBER CAMPS	16/9/16		Moved with No 3 Section R.E. from LATTRE-ST-QUENTIN at 10·30 a.m. arrived HUMBER CAMPS 5·30 p.m. Weather - Bright	
LIGNY-ST-FLOCHEL	17/9/16		Travelled by motor lorries from HUMBER CAMPS at 6·30 a.m. to the 3rd Army School of Trench Mortars at LIGNY-ST-FLOCHEL and started Course in 9·45" Trench Mortars - Weather - Bright	
Do	18/9/16		On Course 9·45" Heavy Trench Mortar. Weather Heavy Rain	
Do	19/9/16		Do Do	
Do	20/9/16		Do Do	
Do	21/9/16		Do Do	
Do	22/9/16		Do 2nd Lieut R.T. MAYLER R.F.A. and Seventeen other ranks arrived & joined Battery on Course. Weather Bright & Sunny	
Do	23/9/16		Course 9·45" Do	
Do	24/9/16		Do Do	
Do	25/9/16		Do Do	
Do	26/9/16		Do Do	
Do	27/9/16		Do Showery	
Do	28/9/16		Do Do	

Sheet 3 to 5 Sheet 5   September   Army Form C. 2118.

WAR DIARY V/33 Heavy Trench Mortar Battery
or
INTELLIGENCE SUMMARY.

Place	Date	Hour	Summary of Events and Information	Remarks and references to Appendices
SOUASTRE	29/9/16		Finished Course. Left School 2-30 p.m. arriving SOUASTRE at 6.30 p.m. Weather fine.	
do	30/9/16		Viewed gun pits and positions in front of FONQUEVILLERS and HEBUTERNE with view to taking over there 9.45 Mustard from Lieut BYWATER of V/46 H.T.M. Battery. Weather fine.	

W.R. Pirnie
Capt R.F.A.
O.C. V/33 H.T.M. Battery

33

WAR DIARY.

X33 T.M. Battery.

September. 1916.

Army Form C. 2118.

WAR DIARY
or
INTELLIGENCE SUMMARY
(Erase heading not required.)

Place	Date	Hour	Summary of Events and Information	Remarks and references to Appendices

Instructions regarding War Diaries and Intelligence Summaries are contained in F. S. Regs., Part II. and the Staff Manual respectively. Title Pages will be prepared in manuscript.

Army Form C. 2118.

WAR DIARY
or
INTELLIGENCE SUMMARY
(Erase heading not required.)

Instructions regarding War Diaries and Intelligence Summaries are contained in F. S. Regs., Part II. and the Staff Manual respectively. Title Pages will be prepared in manuscript.

Place	Date September	Hour	Summary of Events and Information	Remarks and references to Appendices
BECORDEL	1–6th.		Bivouac with D.A.C.	
	6th.		Left BECORDEL. Transport to G.S. Wagons. Personnel marching. Arrived at BONNAY.	
	7th.		Left BONNAY. Arrived at NAOURS.	
	8th.		Left NAOURS. Arrived at BOISBERGUES.	
	9th.		Left BOISBERGUES. Arrived at MILLY in outskirts of DOULLENS.	
	10th.		Left MILLY. Arrived at LATTRE ST. QUENTIN.	
LATTRE ST. QUEN TIN	10–15th		Rested at LATTRE ST. QUENTIN.	
	15th.		Transport of 2 lorries. Proceeded to SOUASTRE.	
	16th.		Arriving about 2 a.m.	
	21st.		Half battery went into action at FONQUEVILLIERS.	
	25th.		Relieved half battery.	
	27th.		Silences issued.	
	29th.		Half battery relieved.	

McPowell Lieut.

2449 Wt. W14957/M90 750,000 1/16 J.B.C. & A. Forms/C.2118/12.

WAR DIARY
or
INTELLIGENCE SUMMARY
(Erase heading not required.)

Army Form C. 2118.

O.C. X33 T.M.B.

Place	Date	Hour	Summary of Events and Information	Remarks and references to Appendices
		21/9/5	Lt. Mackton t.f. R.F.A. was wounded by shrapnel on the 30/9/16. Battery came out of action from Fonquevillers on the 7/10/16. One reinforcement joined unit from 33rd D.A.C. on the 1/10/16. Battery left Souastre 10/10/16 proceeding to Bayencourt. On the 12-13 @ 14/10/16 Battery was employed laying out Trench Mortar ammunition to emplacement in Pedestanes 47034. Gr. Jones G.R. R.G.A. injured cart from Base Hospital 23/10/16. From the 20/10/16 to 27/10/16 Battery was doing fatigues on the communication dumps at Bayencourt. Battery went into action at Hebuterne on the 25/10/16.	Oct 16 32/10.9 Lk.3 18 Kn

– 33 – Y/33 T.M.B Army Form C. 2118.

WAR DIARY
or
INTELLIGENCE SUMMARY

(Erase heading not required.)

Place	Date	Hour	Summary of Events and Information	Remarks and references to Appendices
Brandel	1st		Bivouac with 33rd D.A.C.	
do	Rel/5e			
Bonnay	6th		Marched from Brandel	
Raours	7/t		" " Bonnay	
Boisberques	8t		" " Raours	
Millat	9t		" " Boisberques	
Lattre St Quent	10th		" " Millat	
do	11/14th		Billeted at Lattre St Quentin	
Sonacher	15		From L. St Quentin to	
do	16		Billeted	
do	17		Went over line at Hebuterne	
do	18		In action Hebuterne	
	22		1 Officer & N.C.O proceeded to 3rd Army School to be instructed in Sibees	
	30		Still in action.	

H.Winforke 2/Lt Y33 T.M. Battery
33rd Division

33 Army Form C. 2118.

WAR DIARY
or
INTELLIGENCE SUMMARY
(Erase heading not required.)

Instructions regarding War Diaries and Intelligence Summaries are contained in F. S. Regs., Part II. and the Staff Manual respectively. Title Pages will be prepared in manuscript.

Place	Date	Hour	Summary of Events and Information	Remarks and references to Appendices
BEURDEL	1st to 5th		In bivouac with 32nd D.A.C. — Battery engaged in fatigues	
	6th		Marched to BONNAY	
	7th		" " NAOURS	
	8th		" " BOIS BERGUES	
	9th		" " MILLY	
	10th		" " LATRÉE-ST-QUENTIN	
	11th to 14th		Billets in "	
	15th		By motor lorry to SOUASTRE	
	16th		Reconnoitred line REBUTERNE area.	
	21st		" " BIENVILLERS "	
	22nd		2 officers and 1 N.C.O. to 3rd Army School for instruction in the Trench Mortars	
	16th to 30		Battery billetted at SOUASTRE, engaged in making emplacements in FONCQUVILLERS area	

C.R. Wilkinson
Capt
o/c Z33 T.M.B.

30/9/16

Army Form C. 2118.

Sheets 6 to 8

WAR DIARY V/33 Heavy Trench Mortar Battery

or

~~INTELLIGENCE SUMMARY~~

(Erase heading not required.)

Place	Date	Hour	Summary of Events and Information	Remarks and references to Appendices
SOUASTRE	October 1st		Took over three 9.45" Mortars from 46th Division Heavy T.M. Battery, one gun in front of FONQUEVILLERS and two guns in front of HEBUTERNE. Weather – Fine	
Do	2nd		The whole Battery engaged on clearing guns and improving gun pits & dugouts. Weather Wet.	
Do	3rd		Do	Do
Do	4th		At 12 NOON handed over two guns to the 48th Division Heavy TM Battery, one gun at FONQUEVILLERS and one gun at HEBUTERNE. Weather – Dull	
Do	5th		Battery; removing ammunition from a disused gun position to the position now occupied and improving gun pit and digging dugouts for men. Weather – Rain	
Do	6th		Do	Do
Do	7th		Do	Do
"	8th		"	"
"	9th		"	"
"	10		"	"
BAYENCOURT	11		Personnel of Battery marched from SOUASTRE to BAYENCOURT. Horses "	
"	12		Work on Gun pit in HEBETURNE	
"	13		"	"

Sheets 6 to 8 Sheet 7   October

WAR DIARY V/33 Heavy Trench Mortar Battery

Army Form C. 2118.

or

INTELLIGENCE SUMMARY

Place	Date	Hour	Summary of Events and Information	Remarks and references to Appendices
BAYENCOURT	1916 Oct 14		Work continued on gun pits. Dug out 26 at HEBETURNE	Weather Showery
"	15		" " " "	"
"	16		" " " "	"
"	17		Handed four over mortars in the line to V/48 H.T.M. By	Rain
"	18		Camp fatigues. Drills etc	Rain
"	19		" " " "	Rain
"	20		" " " "	Rain
"	21		" " " "	Fine
"	22		" " " "	Fine
"	23		Captain POWRIE proceeded on leave. 2/Lieut T.R.MAYLER taking over command in his absence.	Weather Rain
"	24		Supplied a working party of 30 other ranks to the 156 Brigade R.F.A. & 10 other ranks to the 152nd Brigade R.F.A. to assist them in constructing their positions. 134896 Gr SIMPSON was killed by a gas shell.	Weather Rain
"	25		Battery continued at work with Brigades	" "
"	26		" " " "	" "

Sheets 6 & 8   Sheet 8   October

Heavy Trench Mortar V/33 Battery

Army Form C. 2118.

WAR DIARY
or
INTELLIGENCE SUMMARY.

(Erase heading not required.)

Instructions regarding War Diaries and Intelligence Summaries are contained in F. S. Regs., Part II. and the Staff Manual respectively. Title pages will be prepared in manuscript.

Place	Date	Hour	Summary of Events and Information	Remarks and references to Appendices
	October 1916			
BAVENCOURT	27"		Battery on fatigue work for R.A Brigades	Rather Keen
	28"		Do	"
	29"		Do	"
	30"		Do	"
	31		Do A further 10 other ranks to 142 B'de R.F.A.	

T. Rossiter Major ~ R.F.A.

For O.C. V/33 H.T.M. Battery

Army Form C. 2118.

1/33 Trench Mortar Battery

WAR DIARY
or
INTELLIGENCE SUMMARY
(Erase heading not required.)

Place	Date	Hour	Summary of Events and Information	Remarks and references to Appendices
SOUASTRE	1/10/16		H Qrs at SOUASTRE from 1st Oct – 11th Oct 1916.	
HEBUTERNE	1/10/16		Battery in action from 1st Oct – 16th Oct 1916	
BAYENCOURT	11/10/16		Left SOUASTRE (evacuated) at BAYENCOURT from 1st Oct to 16th Oct battery working in relief with action at HEBUTERNE	
	16/10/16		Handed over to T.M.By. of 48th Div. & left HEBUTERNE for BAYENCOURT.	
BAYENCOURT	16/10/16		On Dump fatigues from 16th Oct to 19th Oct. Dump work for 33rd D.A.C.	
	20/10/16		20 NCO's and men lent to 162 Brigade R.F.A for digging their rear Gunners at intervals	
	21/10/16		20 NCO's men returned to Battery from 162 Bde RFA after on Dump fatigue	
	25/10/16		Battery on Dump work from 25/10/16 – 31/10/16 awaiting afternoon relief	

M Pelerson Lieut
OC 1/33 T M B 6s

Army Form C. 2118.

WAR DIARY
or
INTELLIGENCE SUMMARY
(Erase heading not required.)

Instructions regarding War Diaries and Intelligence Summaries are contained in F. S. Regs., Part II. and the Staff Manual respectively. Title Pages will be prepared in manuscript.

Place	Date	Hour	Summary of Events and Information	Remarks and references to Appendices
	October 1916			
	1st to 6th		In billets at Souastre — Battery engaged in making emplacements Fonquevillers section.	
	7th		Battery went into action - HEBUTERNE sector.	
	11th		H.Q. transferred to BAYENCOURT, in bivouac.	
	12th to 17th		Battery in action, only registering rounds fired, working on emplacements	
	7th		Came out of action	
	17th - 26th		Assisted B.A.C. at ammunition dump.	
	26th - 31st		Supplies/steepens covering parties for X33 T.M.B	

J.L. Zilfsmith
Capt
OC
X 23 Trench Mortar Battery

Army Form C. 2118.

Sheets 9 & 10

WAR DIARY
or
INTELLIGENCE SUMMARY.
(Erase heading not required.)

V/33 Heavy Trench Mortar B "y"
Sheet 9   November 1916.

Place	Date	Hour	Summary of Events and Information	Remarks and references to Appendices
	1916 Nov			
BAYENCOURT	1		Battery working on fatigues attached to Artillery Brigades in the line	Weather fine
	2		"	"
	3		"	"
	4		"	"
	5		"	"
	6		"	Fine
	7		"	"
	8		"	"
	9		"	Cloudy
	10		"	"
	11		"	Rain
	12		"	"
	13		Men returned from Brigades & worked on B.A.C. Camp	"
	14		"	"
	15		"	"
	16		"	"

Sheets 9 & 10

WAR DIARY V/33 Heavy Trench Mortar Battery

Army Form C. 2118.

Sheet 10

Place	Date	Hour	Summary of Events and Information	Remarks and references to Appendices
BAYENCOURT	1918 Nov 17		Battery at work on D.A.C. Dump.	Winter Line
	18		" " " " "	"
	19		" " " " "	"
	20		" " " " "	Rain
	21		" " " " "	"
TALMAS	22		Battery moved from BAYENCOURT to TALMAS by Motor Lorries	Line
BAILLEUL	23		" " " TALMAS to BAILLEUL " " "	"
	24		" engaged on salvage of enemy material	"
	25		" " " " " "	"
ORÉVILLERS	26		" moved from BAILLEUL to ORÉVILLERS HAMEL Capt C.W.BRIE appointed Town Mayor
HAMEL			of HAIRAINES whilst the Division is in this district, 2nd Lieut J.R.MAYLER took command of the Battery. 2nd Lieut F.C.C. MANLEY acting Town Mayor of ORÉVILLERS HAMEL.	Line
	27		Battery engaged on Dells, Physical Training &c.	"
	28		" " " " "	"
	29		" " " " "	"
	30		" " " " "	"

T. Oswald Mayler Capt R.A.
V/33 Heavy T.M.B.Y.

WAR DIARY or INTELLIGENCE SUMMARY

(Erase heading not required.)

Army Form C. 2118.

T M Bty 3
Vol 4

Place	Date	Hour	Summary of Events and Information	Remarks and references to Appendices
	Nov 1-10		Battery employed making gun positions in Hamel Street off Jean Bapt. Very difficult work owing to the state of the trenches.	
			B.O. transferred on 3/11 to sap leading to T.M.S. gun position in Hamel St.	
	Nov 5		One officer and party from 1st Brigade R.F.A.	
	Nov 11		One man killed by shell in Jean Bapt. Second on round turning relieved	
			Battery employed filling up ammunition to positions.	
	Nov 11-13			
	Nov 13		Three guns in action. First fifteen rounds one gun out of action after first round.	
	Nov 15		Battery returned to Bivouac at Bayencourt.	
	Nov 22		Bivouaced at 10-10 A.M. arrived Fienvillers 2-0 P.M.	
	Nov 23		Left Fienvillers 9-0 A.M. arrived Brailly 1-30 P.M.	
	Nov 26		Left Brailly 10-o'clock military convoy Le Hamel 4 P.M.	

W Nicholson
For O.C. X33 T.M.B.

Army Form C. 2118.

/33 T M Bty

WAR DIARY
or
INTELLIGENCE SUMMARY

(Erase heading not required.)

1st month of November 1916.

Place	Date	Hour	Summary of Events and Information	Remarks and references to Appendices
BAYENCOURT	1st to 11th		Under Canvas. On the Ammunition Dump. Fatigue work.	
"	12th		One NCO & six men lent to X Battery as a carrying party. One party at 10 AM took parts at 6 pm to Linden in HEBUTERNE. These parties carried trench mortar ammunition.	
"	"			
"	18th/11		Our client fatigues for 33rd D.A.C.	
"	9th		Lent to X Bty	
"	19th			
"	23rd		2/Lt. T. WINGATE for TALMAS.	
"	"		Left BAYENCOURT for TALMAS.	
TALMAS	25th		Arrived from BAYENCOURT.	
"	25th		Left TALMAS for BAILLEUL	
BAILLEUL	25th		Arrived from TALMAS	
"	2nd		Cleaning guns & equipment	
DREUIL-LE HAMEL	26th		Left BAILLEUL for DREUIL - LE HAMEL & Arrived from BAILLEUL. In rest billets	
"	26-30		Physical drill, gun drill, cleaning equipment, lectures on Aero Sights. Football Tournament in the afternoon.	

1/12/16. A Nicholson Lt
O.C. /33 T M Bty

Hdqrs 33rd D.A.

Trench War Diary
of Y/33 T.M. Battery

11/7/16

[signature]
MAJOR, R.A.
BRIGADE MAJOR 33rd DIVISIONAL ARTILLERY.
for BRIGADIER GENERAL, R.A.
COMMANDING 33rd DIVISIONAL ARTILLERY.

WAR DIARY
INTELLIGENCE SUMMARY
(Erase heading not required.)

Army Form C. 2118.

Place	Date	Hour	Summary of Events and Information	Remarks and references to Appendices
November	1916			
	1st–11th		Battery in bivouac at BAVENCOURT. Engaged in trench fatigues for X33 T.M.B.	
	12th–13th		OC fitting & riding men in HEBUTERNE with one gun ready to go forward in action (not ordered eventually)	
	13th–28th		Assisting D.A.C. on BAVENCOURT dump.	
	22nd		By motor lorry to TALMAS, in billets there for one night.	
	23rd		" " to BAILLEUL, " " 3 "	
	26th		Marched to LE HAMEL.	
	26th–29th		Billets in " " an rest. Physical training esp. gun etc drill carried out.	

L. A. Hitchcock
Capt
OC
Z 33 Trench Mortar Battery

Sheets 11 to 13

WAR DIARY or INTELLIGENCE SUMMARY

Army Form C. 2118.

1/33 Heavy Trench Mortar Battery. Vol 5

Place	Date	Hour	Summary of Events and Information	Remarks and references to Appendices
DREUIL LE HAMEL	1/12/16		Inspection by General Pinney and Blano	Weather Fine
Do	2/12/16		Training. Physical, marching, rifle drill etc	" Dull
Do	3/12/16		Do	" Rain
Do	4/12/16		Do	" Fine
Do	5/12/16		Do	" Dull
Do	6/12/16		Do	" Misty
Do	7/12/16		Do	" Rain
Do	8/12/16		Do	" Fine
Do	9/12/16		Do	" Fine
Do	10/12/16		Do	" Fine
CAMP No 12.	11/12/16		Moved by Motor Lorry to No.12 Camp	" Fine
ERRY-SUR-	12/12/16		Do	" Fine
SOMME	13/12/16		Do	" Rain
Do	14/12/16		Moved to Camp No 14 (next camp.) Capt Dorrie appointed Command't No 14 Camp	" Fine
Do	15/12/16		NCO's and men employed clearing camp and burying dead animal	Rain

Sheet 11 to 13

WAR DIARY
or
INTELLIGENCE SUMMARY

Army Form C. 2118.

V/33 HEAVY TRENCH MORTAR BATTERY

Sheet 12

Place	Date	Hour	Summary of Events and Information	Remarks and references to Appendices
No 14 Camp	16/12/16		NCO's and men employed cleaning and repairing Camp & Huts	Weather – Rain
BRAY-SUR-SOMME	17/12/16		Do	" Snow
"	18/12/16		Do	" Rain
Do	19/12/16		Do	" Rain
Do	20/12/16		Do	" Fine
Do	21/12/16		Do	" Fine
Do	22/12/16		10 ORs sent to HQ RA for working party to 18 pr Brigade remainder on cleaning Camp	" Rain
Do	23/12/16		Cleaning Camp	" Rain
Do	24/12/16		Do	" Rain
Do	25/12/16		Do	"V. Dull
Do	26/12/16		10 ORs returned from HQRA	" Rain
VAUX-EN-AMIENOIS	27/12/16		Battery received 25 men from 33 DTMB for course in Heavy Trench Mortar and the whole proceeded to HQ Army Trench Mortar School – Fine	– Fine
Do	28/12/16		Drill and instruction at School	– Fine
Do	29/12/16		Do	– Fine

Army Form C. 2118.

Feb 11 to 13

WAR DIARY V/33 HEAVY TRENCH
or
INTELLIGENCE SUMMARY. MORTAR BATTERY

(Erase heading not required.)

Sheet no 13

Instructions regarding War Diaries and Intelligence Summaries are contained in F. S. Regs., Part II. and the Staff Manual respectively. Title pages will be prepared in manuscript.

Place	Date	Hour	Summary of Events and Information	Remarks and references to Appendices
VAUX-EN-	11/2/16		Drill & instruction at 1st Army School of Mortars, fired 7 rounds	
AMIENOIS	13/2/16		with new charge 7 to give a more accurate and alerting moment. Unable to carry on to weather. Weather - Rain, bad light and a gale of wind.	

W.T. Powrie
Capt. R.F.A.
O C V/33 H.T.M. Battery

Army Form C. 2118.

WAR DIARY
or
INTELLIGENCE SUMMARY
(Erase heading not required.)

Place	Date	Hour	Summary of Events and Information	Remarks and references to Appendices
Le Nomel			From 1st – 31st. Battery out on rest.	
"	2.12.16.		One reinforcement joined the Battery from 156 Brigade R.F.A.	
"	3.12.16.		Four reinforcements joined the Battery from 33rd D.A.C.	
"	4.12.16.		One officer joined the Battery from 166 Brigade. R.F.A.	
"	From 1st – 31st/12	From 9 a.m. to 10 a.m.	Physical exercises.	
		" 11 a.m. to 12 a.m.	Gun drill, rifle exercises, or route march.	
			On every third day – three men of the Battery on fatigues at baths in Avaines.	
			One bathing parade each week.	

C.L. Lockwood
Capt
3/12/16 OC. X33. T.M.B.

# Army Form C. 2118.

WAR DIARY
or
INTELLIGENCE SUMMARY

(Erase heading not required.)

Place	Date	Hour	Summary of Events and Information	Remarks and references to Appendices
DREUIL LE HAMEL	1/12/16 to 31/12/16		Line occupied in training	

H Winfale
Lieut R.F.A.
f. O.C. Y33 T.M.Battery

Army Form C. 2118.

WAR DIARY
or
INTELLIGENCE SUMMARY
(Erase heading not required.)

Instructions regarding War Diaries and Intelligence Summaries are contained in F. S. Regs., Part II. and the Staff Manual respectively. Title Pages will be prepared in manuscript.

Place	Date	Hour	Summary of Events and Information	Remarks and references to Appendices
December 1916	1st – 31st		Battery in rest at DREUIL-HAMEL. Programme of training carried out. Physical Training – Route marches.	
	"	"	Instruction in cutting and laying panel, Dial sights, clynometers etc. Close order and rifle drill.	
	"	"	17 men from No 3 Sec D.A.C. trained in 2" French Mortar. 25 rounds were obtained and these men instructed in firing.	
	2nd – 7th		Practice in revolver shooting.	
	24th		No. 20530 Dr. R.C. Chamberlain died.	
	27th – 31st		General supplies for R.E. stores at AIRAINES station until handed over to Major.	

J.L. Fitzgerald
Capt
OC
L 33 T.M.B.

SHEETS 1 to 15

WAR DIARY V/33 HEAVY TRENCH MORTAR BATTERY
Army Form C. 2118.

or

INTELLIGENCE SUMMARY.

(Erase heading not required.)

SHEET No. 1th   Vol 6

Instructions regarding War Diaries and Intelligence Summaries are contained in F. S. Regs., Part II. and the Staff Manual respectively. Title pages will be prepared in manuscript.

Place	Date	Hour	Summary of Events and Information	Remarks and references to Appendices
VAUX-EN-AMIENOIS	1/1/17		At 4th Army School of Mortars — Fired 8 rounds good results Weather Fine	
Do	2/1/17		Drill and instruction — " Fine	
"	3/1/17		Do " Fine	
"	4/1/17		Do " Fine	
LONGPRÉ-LES-CORPS-SAINTS	5/1/17		Left 4th Army School of Instruction of Gunnery and travelled by motor lorry to Bullets in Lonspré arriving 3 p.m. Weather Fine.	
Do	6/1/17		Drill etc, and washing parties " Rain	
"	7/1/17		" " Fine	
"	8/1/17		" " Rain	
"	9/1/17		" " Wet & Rain	
"	10/1/17		" " Cold & Dull	
"	11/1/17		" " Cold & Dull	
"	12/1/17		" one man to Hospital with measles. consequently " Dull & Fine	
"	13/1/17		Battery is put by M.O. into isolation " Rain	
"	14/1/17		Drill etc " "snow, very cold"	

WAR DIARY V/33 HEAVY TRENCH MORTAR BATTERY

Army Form C. 2118.

SHEETS 14 to 15

INTELLIGENCE SUMMARY.

SHEET No 15

Place	Date	Hour	Summary of Events and Information	Remarks and references to Appendices
LONGPRES-lès-S	15/1/17		Drill etc one more man to Hospital with measles	Weather bright & cold
"	16/1/17		" Battery placed in quarantine on o/c measles	"
"	17/1/17		"	" Snow
"	18/1/17		"	" Sleet, Rain
"	19/1/17		"	" Cold, dull
"	20/1/17		"	" Cold, windy
"	21/1/17		"	" Very cold
"	22/1/17		"	"
"	23/1/17		"	"
"	24/1/17		"	" Freezing
"	25/1/17		"	"
"	26/1/17		"	"
"	27/1/17		"	"
"	28/1/17		"	"
"	29/1/17		"	"
"	30/1/17		"	"
"	31/1/17		"	"

WAR DIARY
or
INTELLIGENCE SUMMARY
(Erase heading not required.)

Army Form C. 2118.

X33 TMB

Place	Date	Hour	Summary of Events and Information	Remarks and references to Appendices
Le Hamel	From 1.1.17 to 4.1.17		Battery employed on fatigues at railway station in Amiens. Battery supplied guard over R.E. Stores at this place.	
	4.1.17		Left Le Hamel for Longpré-les-corps-saints, arriving there at 3.30 P.m.	
Longpré	5.1.17 to 7.1.17		Parades each day. – Physical exercises, route marches and gun drill.	
Vaux	7.1.17 to 17.1.17		Left Longpré for 4th Army School of Mortars. Parades 8.30 A.m. to 12.30 P.m. – Practical instructions on 2" French Howitzers. 1.30 P.m. to 4.00 P.m. Lectures on 2" Howitzers and ammunition.	
Longpré	18.1.17 to 23.1.17		Battery left 4th Army School and arrived at Longpré-les-corps-saints. Parades each day. – Physical exercises, route marches and gun drill.	
	23.1.17		Battery left Longpré for Fresse.	
Fresse	27.1.17		Battery went into action with one gun.	
	31.1.17		Employed on digging gun emplacements and a dug-out.	

O.C. X.33. T.M.B.

Army Form C. 2118.

WAR DIARY
or
INTELLIGENCE SUMMARY
(Erase heading not required.)

V/33 T M Battery

Summary of Events and Information

Place	Date	Hour	Summary of Events and Information	Remarks and references to Appendices
DREUIL	1-1-19		In training up to 4-1-19	
-Do-	4-1-19		Moved to LONGPRE-LES-CORPS-SAINTS	
LONGPRE	5-1-19		In training up to 25-1-19	
-Do-	25-1-19		Moved to 4th Army forward area @ FRISE	
FRISE	25-1-19		Settled up shelters for members	
FRISE	28-1-19		Went into action which of BOUCHAVESNES -80 - 80 - -	
TRENCHES	29-1-19		Making Emplacements -80 - 80 - -	
-Do-	31-1-19			

31/1/19

A.J. Rodgers for Lieut. R.G.A.
2 I/C V/33 T M Bg.

Army Form C. 2118.

WAR DIARY
or
INTELLIGENCE SUMMARY
(Erase heading not required.)

Instructions regarding War Diaries and Intelligence Summaries are contained in F. S. Regs., Part II. and the Staff Manual respectively. Title Pages will be prepared in manuscript.

Place	Date	Hour	Summary of Events and Information	Remarks and references to Appendices
	January 1917			
	1st – 4th		Battery in billets at BREVIL. Programme of training carried out.	
	4th		Moved by motor lorry to LONGPRÉ-LES-CORPS-SAINTS.	
	8th – 13th		12 Men from 3 Bdn DAC trained in 2" T.M. 12 men from Battery went to DAC to replace these men. Course for another 12 men commenced but not completed owing to departure of 3 Bde DAC.	
	14th		O.C. Battery went forward to take over emplacements, dug outs etc. from trench mortar to reconnoitre line.	
	19th		Battery moved forward from LONGPRÉ by motor lorry to FRISE BEND.	
	25th			
	25th – 31st		Fatigue & ration parties provided for X 33 T.M.B.	

C. L. Fitzgerald
Capt
OC
X 33 T.M. Battery

2449 Wt. W14957/M90 750,000 1/16 J.B.C. & A. Forms/C.2118/12.

SHEETS 16 to 18

WAR DIARY V/33 HEAVY TRENCH
or
INTELLIGENCE SUMMARY. MORTAR BATTERY.

SHEET 16   Vol 7

Army Form C. 2118.

Place	Date	Hour	Summary of Events and Information	Remarks and references to Appendices
LONGPRÉ-LES-CORPS-SAINTS	1/2/17		Drill etc	
"	2/2/17		"	Weather freezing
"	3/2/17		Battery weekly programme followed from preceeding "	"
"	4/2/17		"	"
FRISE	5/2/17		Moved by train to FRISE — MAP AMIENS 17 1/40,000 — D.1 — and took over two 9.45" Trench Mortars which had been delivered pending arrival of Battery. Weather - snow - freezing	
"	6/2/17		Cleaning guns and Dugouts out and generally settling down & preparing for action — freezing	
"	7/2/17		Building gun emplacement in line at — MAP — PERONNE, 62cNW 4, Edition 3A. 1/10000 — H,12,d,74,82	
"	8/2/17		2nd Lieut M. HOWELL joined Battery posted on from 7th inst. freezing	
"	9/2/17		Do	Do
"	10/2/17		Two more guns received from Ordnance. Building gun emplacement & dugouts in line	Do
"	11/2/17		Building gun emplacement & dugouts in line	Do
"	12/2/17		Do	Do
"	13/2/17		Two guns received on 10th sent to 5th Army School of Mortars on loan	Do
"	14/2/17		Fired test rounds between 9-30 and 9-50 p.m. in support of Infantry raid. Nothing of interest to report.	Do

SHEETS 16 to 18

Instructions regarding War Diaries and Intelligence
Summaries are contained in F. S. Regs., Part II.
and the Staff Manual respectively. Title pages
will be prepared in manuscript.

WAR DIARY V/33 HEAVY TRENCH MORTAR BATTERY

or INTELLIGENCE SUMMARY.

(Erase heading not required.)

Army Form C. 2118.

SHEET 17

Place	Date	Hour	Summary of Events and Information	Remarks and references to Appendices
FRISE	14/2/17		Nothing of interest to record	Frosty
"	15/2/17		Fired two Rounds.	Slight thaw during evening
"	16/2/17		Fired two Rounds: the elevating handle got bent, apparently by the shock of discharge. Handles + spindle from the other gun were fitted + gun put in action	— Cold fine
"	17/2/17		Nothing of interest to report. Building gun emplacement.	Thaw fine
"	18/2/17		Do	Thaw fine
"	19/2/17		Do	Frosty fine
"	20/2/17		Do	Thaw fine
"	21/2/17		Do	Thaw misty, Damp
"	22/2/17		Do	Thaw misty
"	23/2/17		Fired four rounds. Took over from V/4 H.T.M.Bty one gun in emplacement. Gun said to be ready to fire but will require a week in the dry hard work to get ready for action. Map reference of gun TRENCH. MAP. FRANCE. SHEET 62C NW. EDITION 3. B.20.c.7.6. C.20.C.7.6.	Thaw misty
"	24/2/17		Nothing to record	Damp sleety
"	25/2/17		Do except two rounds fired registration	Do
"	26/2/17		Do	Fine

WAR DIARY or **INTELLIGENCE SUMMARY**

SHEETS 16 to 18

V/33 HEAVY TRENCH MORTAR BATTERY

SHEET 18

Place	Date	Hour	Summary of Events and Information	Remarks and references to Appendices
FRISE	27/2/17		Fired ten rounds in Infantry raid, four men wounded	Fire
"	29/2/17		Nothing of interest to report	Drill

W.K Pound
Capt. R.F.A.
OC V/33 H.T.M.B5
1/3/17

Army Form C. 2118.

WAR DIARY
or
INTELLIGENCE SUMMARY
(Erase heading not required.)

X 33 T.M.B.
28.2.17

Place	Date	Hour	Summary of Events and Information	Remarks and references to Appendices
	Jan. 1st–5th		Battery in line preparing positions for four guns.	
			All guns ready for action on night of the 5th.	
	Feb. 6th		Half battery returned to Suez Middills.	
	"	10th	Two detachments in line relieved by remainder.	
	"	10th–14th	Engaged wire-cutting. About 150 rounds fired at enemy wire. Satisfactory report received from infantry patrol	
	Feb. 15th		Half battery in line relieved by L 33 T.M.B.	
	"	17th	Lt. 16 A.D. Malcolm wounded while temporarily serving with L 33 T.M.B.	
			(afterwards reported died of wounds)	
			Gun detachments carry out daily Sanitary Fatigue, gas helmet and rifle inspection.	
	Feb. 19th		Two detachments went into line. Guns ready for action. All personnel ordered for firing cancelled. Guns and detachments withdrawn.	
	"	20th	Two detachments returned to billets.	
	"	21st–26th	Parades daily at 10.00 A.M. Rifles, gas-helmets and box respirators inspected. Three detachments consisting of three N.C.O's and eight men went into line to prepare for action. One gun registered on night of 27th.	
	Feb. 28th		All guns registered — awaiting orders.	

Army Form C. 2118.

WAR DIARY
or
INTELLIGENCE SUMMARY

(Erase heading not required.)

Instructions regarding War Diaries and Intelligence Summaries are contained in F. S. Regs., Part II. and the Staff Manual respectively. Title Pages will be prepared in manuscript.

Place	Date	Hour	Summary of Events and Information	Remarks and references to Appendices
Trenches	1/2/17	—	In action in line in front of Beaumont and withdrew on relief 15/2/17	
Trenches	15/2/17	—	Have come out of line, going on support of second line	
Trenches	16/2/17	—	16/2/17 to be prepared	
Trenches	17/2/17	—	Prepared guns for new concentration	
Trenches	18/2/17	—	Stood to arms	
Trenches	19/2/17	—	Moved in action, prepared to move everything now more	
Trenches	20/2/17	—	Moved the guns for bombardment to support and	
	21/2/17	—	Stood on alert	
	22/2/17	—	Came out of action to rest billets in forward area.	
	25/2/17	—		
	26/2/17	—		
	27/2/17	—		
	28/2/17	—	Parades and training at rest billet.	

W. Middleton
Lt.Col/133.T.M.B.

2449 Wt. W14957/M90 750,000 1/16 J.B.C. & A. Forms/C.2118/12.

Army Form C. 2118.

WAR DIARY
or
INTELLIGENCE SUMMARY
(Erase heading not required.)

Instructions regarding War Diaries and Intelligence Summaries are contained in F. S. Regs., Part II. and the Staff Manual respectively. Title Pages will be prepared in manuscript.

Place	Date	Hour	Summary of Events and Information	Remarks and references to Appendices
	February.	1914.		
Hill	1-12th		Training Gun Emplacements. Clerg.	
Bend.	13th.		One section in action. Right sector	
	14th-18th		Fatigues and return carrying for section in action.	
	19th-28th		Battery in action.	

Wingate H/t
for O.C. 227 T M By

2449 Wt. W14957/M90 750,000 1/16 J.B.C. & A. Forms/C.2118/12.

Sheets 19 to 20

WAR DIARY
or
INTELLIGENCE SUMMARY.

Army Form C. 2118.

V/33 Heavy Trench Mortar Battery

Sheet 19 &

Place	Date	Hour	Summary of Events and Information	Remarks and references to Appendices
Friss	March 1		Nothing of interest to report	Weather Cold
"	2		"	" Fine
"	3		"	" Fine
"	4		"	" Fine
"	5		"	" Snow
"	6		"	" Fine
"	7		"	"
"	8		Found transport over to V/40	"
"	9		Checking equipment & packing stores	"
"	10		"	"
"	11		Move to BAILLY LE SEC by lorries	"
Bailly le Sec	12		Physical Training - Rifle & Revolver Practice	"
"	13		"	"
"	14		"	"
"	15		"	"
"	16		"	"
"	17		"	"
"	18		"	"
"	19		"	"
"	20		"	"

Sheet 20

WAR DIARY
or
INTELLIGENCE SUMMARY.

Army Form C. 2118.

V/33 Heavy Trench Mortar Battery

Sheets 19 to 20

(Erase heading not required.)

Place	Date	Hour	Summary of Events and Information	Remarks and references to Appendices
SAILLY-LE-SEC	March 21 1917		Physical Training. Rifle & Revolver Shooting etc.	Weather fine
"	22		" " " "	"
"	23		" " " "	"
"	24		" " " "	"
"			proceeded on leave 2/Lt T.R. MAYLER took over command	" Captain POWRIE
"	25		Moved by lorries to NAOURS	"
NAOURS	26		Battery resting	"
"	27		Moved by lorries to MEZEROLLES	"
MEZEROLLES	28		" " " BOURET-SUR-CANCHE	
BOURET-SUR-CANCHE	29		" " " ARRAS	
ARRAS	30		Cleaning kits etc	
ARRAS	31		Took over two Mortars from V/15 one at G23 c25.3 (1 by ARRAS Sheet 1/10,000) and one in damaged pit at G23 d0.9.9.	

T. Rooster Mayler 2/Lt R.F.A.
for OC V/33 H T M Bty

Army Form C. 2118.

WAR DIARY
or
INTELLIGENCE SUMMARY
(Erase heading not required.)

Instructions regarding War Diaries and Intelligence Summaries are contained in F. S. Regs., Part II. and the Staff Manual respectively. Title Pages will be prepared in manuscript.

31. 3. 17.

Place	Date	Hour	Summary of Events and Information	Remarks and references to Appendices
Suzanne	1.3.17		Battery in action with four guns. Three detachments in trenches.	
	2.3.17		4 Btty rounds fired at enemy's men.	
	3.3.17		Battery relieved by Y/53 T.M. Battery.	
	4.3.17		Baths at Suzanne.	
	6.3.17		Brought guns, stores, etc. out of the line.	
	7.3.17		Parades as follows – 8.00 a.m. – 2.30 a.m. Physical exercises.	
			9.00 a.m. – 10.00 a.m. Rifle inspection and marching drill. Box respirators inspection.	
	11.3.17		Left Suzanne at 9.00 a.m. and arrived at Sailly-Le-Sec 3.00 p.m.	
Sailly-Le-Sec	12.3.17 – 24.3.17		Parades each day as follows – 9.00 a.m. – 9.30 a.m. Physical exercises.	
			10.00 a.m. – 12.00 m. Tactical schemes on Trench Mortars, or route march.	
			2.00 p.m. – 3.00 p.m. Inspection of box respirators, rifles – marching drill.	
			Four men from D.A.C. temporarily attached to battery for instruction.	
	25.3.17		Left Sailly-Le-Sec 9.00 a.m. and arrived at "Naours" at 2.00 p.m.	
Naours	26.3.17		Left Naours 6.00 a.m. arriving at Hezerolles at 2.30 p.m.	
Hezerolles	27.3.17		Left Hezerolles 1.00 p.m. and arrived at Bouet-sur-Canche at 6.00 p.m.	
Bouet-sur-Canche	28.3.17		Left Bouet-sur-Canche at 6.00 a.m. arriving at Arras at 7.30 p.m.	
Arras	31.3.17		Battery went into trenches with four guns.	

M Paw b R.F.A.
O.C. 153 Trench Mortar Battery.

WAR DIARY
or
INTELLIGENCE SUMMARY

Y33 Trench Mortar Battery

Place	Date	Hour	Summary of Events and Information	Remarks and references to Appendices
FRIEZE	1/3/17		Battery in action in Clery Sector.	
	8/3/17		Relieved in trenches.	
	11/3/17		Left Frieze for Sailly-le-Sec.	
	15/3/17		Training at Sailly-le-Sec	
	16/4/17		" " " "	
	23/3/17		Left Sailly-le-Sec for Naours.	
	26/3/17		Inspection & Cleaning Fatigues	
	27/3/17		Left Naours for Mezerolles.	
	28/3/17		" " Mezerolles for Frevent.	
	29/3/17		" " Frevent for Arras	
	30/3/17		Inspection of positions in trenches at Arras	
ARRAS	31/3/17		Battery in action BLANGY SECTOR	

H Winfield
Lieut R.F.A.
O.C. Y33 T M Battery

Army Form C. 2118.

WAR DIARY
or
INTELLIGENCE SUMMARY
(Erase heading not required.)

Y/33 TRENCH MORTAR BATTERY.

Instructions regarding War Diaries and Intelligence Summaries are contained in F. S. Regs., Part II. and the Staff Manual respectively. Title Pages will be prepared in manuscript.

Place	Date	Hour	Summary of Events and Information	Remarks and references to Appendices
D17a 55.30 Sheet 28 NE1	1/3/17		Ref. emplacements & pit huts mortars in action.	
D17c 40.80 Sheet 28 NE1	31/3/17		Took two mortars over from X33 T.M.Battery	
			Have mortars now in action firing on S.O.S.	

U. Winfate
Capt. R.F.A.
O.C. Y33 T.M.Battery.

2449 Wt. W14957/M90 750,000 1/16 J.B.C. & A. Forms/C.2118/12.

Army Form C. 2118.

WAR DIARY
or
INTELLIGENCE SUMMARY

T.M.B.g Vol 8

(Erase heading not required.)

Instructions regarding War Diaries and Intelligence Summaries are contained in F.S. Regs., Part II. and the Staff Manual respectively. Title Pages will be prepared in manuscript.

33

Place	Date	Hour	Summary of Events and Information	Remarks and references to Appendices
Aveluy Sector	1/3/17 to 8/3/17		Battery in action at Courcy.	
Forur Pund	9/3/17		Removing guns from the trenches	
Souastre	11th		Battery moved to Sailly le Sec.	
"	12th			
"	13th 14th		Route marching, musketry practice & gun drill	
Naours	26th 27th		" billets at Naours	
Hezerolles	28th		" Hezerolles	
Bonnet sur Cenel	9/4		" Bonnet sur Cancle.	
Arras	29th 30th		" at Arras	
"	31st		Billet fatigues & guards.	

J. Jones ?Lt R.F.A.
O.C. 233 T.M.B.

2449 Wt. W14957/Mgo 750,000 1/16 J.B.C. & A. Forms/C.2118/12.

WAR DIARY Army Form C. 2118.
INTELLIGENCE SUMMARY
(Erase heading not required.)

V/33 HEAVY TRENCH MORTAR BATTERY

Sheet 21
April 1917 Vol 9

Place	Date	Hour	Summary of Events and Information	Remarks and references to Appendices
AREAS	April 1st	2 pm	Fired ten rounds on BLANGY Island, G21a with (Reg Corr Shet 1: 10,000, North Section Lens) account mortar into position G.23 & G.25.25	
	" 2nd		Fired twenty rounds on BLANGY Island – support trenches S6 in G.24a	"
	" 3		" " " " " " " " " " " " "	"
	" 4		Left " " " " " " " " " " " Gun	"
	" 5		Gun temporarily put out of action by shell set in adjoined trench	"
	" 6		Left Gun opened on BLANGY Island. the Both mortars again in action	"
	" 7		Thirty " " " " " " Capt W.L. Powell E. returned from leave	" Heavy
	" 8		" " " " " " " " " returned command	"
	" 9		Fifty rounds at a.m. on no support trenches in G.24 a.	" of the battery
	" 10		One mortar taken out of position & fetched back to Billets	" Less
	" 11		" " " " " " " " " " " "	" "
	" 12		Our bursting mortars etc	" Rain

Army Form C. 2118.

Sheet 22.

WAR DIARY
or
INTELLIGENCE SUMMARY.

V/33 HEAVY TRENCH MORTAR BATTERY

(Erase heading not required.)

Month 21 to 22

Place	Date	Hour	Summary of Events and Information	Remarks and references to Appendices
ARRAS	April 13 1917		Dismantling old gun positions in ARRAS	Weather Rain
	14		" " " " " " "	" Fine
	15		" " " " " " "	" "
	16		" " " " " " "	" "
	17		Making tracks from ARRAS cavalry to gun positions through old trench system	" Rain
	18		" " " " " " " "	" Snow
	19		" " " " " " " "	" Rain
	20		" " " " " " " "	" "
	21		" " " " " " " "	" "
	22		" " " " " " " "	" Fine
	23		Ditto	" "
	24		" 1 N.C.O. 15 men on route fatigue	" "
	25		" 1 N.C.O. ten men to 33. D.A.C. of FEUCHY Dump	" "
	26		" " " " "	" "
	27		" " " " "	" "
	28		" " " " "	" "
	29		" " " " "	" "
	30		" " " " "	" "

/ Robert Maybe 2nd R.G.A.
Lieut V/33 Heavy Trench
Mortar Battery

Army Form C. 2118.

WAR DIARY
or
INTELLIGENCE SUMMARY
(Erase heading not required.)

1/33 TMB. 30-4-17

X/33 TRENCH MORTAR BATTERY.

Instructions regarding War Diaries and Intelligence Summaries are contained in F. S. Regs., Part II. and the Staff Manual respectively. Title Pages will be prepared in manuscript.

Place	Date	Hour	Summary of Events and Information	Remarks and references to Appendices
Arras	1-4-17		Battery in the line preparing positions and getting ammunition up to positions.	
Blangy	2-4-17		Battery in action	
	3-4-17		Fired 70 rounds into front post.	
	4-4-17		Fired 100 rounds enemy's wire	
	5-4-17		Fired 50 " enemy's support line. The gunners wounded whilst firing	
	6-4-17		Night " "	
	7-4-17		Fired 130 rounds at enemy's support line.	
	8-4-17		— 180 — wire	
	9-4-17		— 80 — communication trenches	
	10-4-17		The battery moved to billets in Arras. Were given an N.E.S. and an own. Building bridges over trenches for use at attack.	
Arras	11-4-17	9 A.M. & 12 HHE Enemy had damaged two our guns put	
	12-4-17 to 15-4-17		R.F.O. and Zero hour works on our billets positions at L top of square.	
	16 & 25-4-17 29 - 30-4-17	10-30 A.M.	The five puffs and clay making. Idy up shell belts and heads. Five postition & Sect refreshed in L2.	

2449 Wt. W14957/M90 750,000 1/16 J.B.C. & A. Forms/C.2118/12.

Army Form C. 2118.

Y33 TRENCH MORTAR BATTERY

WAR DIARY or INTELLIGENCE SUMMARY

(Erase heading not required.)

Place	Date	Hour	Summary of Events and Information	Remarks and references to Appendices
ARRAS	1.4.17			
	9.4.17		Battery in action BLANGY SECTOR.	
	10.4.17		Battery employed on fatigues	
	30.4.17		and road making.	

Thingate
Lieut. R.F.A.
O.C. Y33. T.M. Bty.

Army Form C. 2118.

WAR DIARY
or
INTELLIGENCE SUMMARY
(Erase heading not required.)

2/33 TMB

Place	Date	Hour	Summary of Events and Information	Remarks and references to Appendices
April 917				
A.R.S	1st &5th		Battery engaged in carrying ammunition to batteries in X-Y/33 T.M. B's	
	8th		Am. filled being position at X of Epehy in action at Y.32	
	9th		Entire movement party from trenches	
	13th-14th		engaged in dismantling duffla mounts	
	16th-25th		and making an emplacement with X.M.V Batteries	
	29th-30th		Part of battery ammunition fatigue for V.M. B's stokes mortars	
			New Emplts from rested R.S. and R.H. Dustan mounted	
			Emm mountings & stores completed. All have follow wire deflection scale & handles	

E.L. Ashhead
Capt
OC
2/33 T.M.B

Sheets 23 to 24.

WAR DIARY
or
INTELLIGENCE SUMMARY.

V/33 Heavy Trench Mortar Battery

Army Form C. 2118.

Sheet 23   Vol 10

Place	Date 1917	Hour	Summary of Events and Information	Remarks and references to Appendices
ARRAS	MAR 1		Battery at Cmtts i/c - one NCO & ten men at Feuchy Dump	
	2		" " " " " " " " " " " "	
	3		" " " " " " " " " " " "	
	4		" " " " " " " " " " " "	
	5		" " " " " " " " " " " "	
	6		" " " " " " " " " " " "	
	7		" " " " " " " " " " " "	
	8		" " " " " " " " " " " "	
	9		" " " " " " " " " " " "	
	10		BENTLEY W.L. was specially commended by O/C 186" Brigade R.F.A. for excellent work done when acting as Telephonist to the F.O.O. of that Brigade during an attack. No 168533 Gr.	
	11		Cmtts i/c One NCO & 15 men at FEUCHY DUMP 2/LIEUT ARTHUR HEADS M.G. R.F.A (X/33TMB 5) took command vice Capt W.L. POWRIE R.F.A attached to 33 C.A.C.	
	12		Cmtts i/c One NCO & ten men at FEUCHY DUMP	
	13		" " " " " " " " " " " "	
	14		" " " " " " " " " " " "	
	15		" " " " " " " " " " " "	
	16		" " " " " " " " " " " "	

Army Form C. 2118.

Sheet 23624

WAR DIARY
or
INTELLIGENCE SUMMARY.

(Erase heading not required.)

V/33 HEAVY TRENCH MORTAR BATTERY

Sheet 24

Place	Date 1917	Hour	Summary of Events and Information	Remarks and references to Appendices
ARRAS	MAY 17		Drills etc. One NCO 6 men at FEUCHY Dump	
	18		"	
	19		" NCO & ten men to 162 B" R.G.A. H.Qrs.	
	20		" " " " "	
	21		" " " " "	
	22		" " " " "	
	23		" " " " "	
	24		" " " " "	
	25		" " " " "	
	26		" " " " "	
	27		" " " " "	
	28		" " " " "	
	29		" " " " "	
	30		" " " " "	
	31		Lt A. HEARD M.C. proceeded to 3rd Army School of Mortars on O.T.M. O'course 2 Lt T. D. MAYLER R.F.A. assumed command of the Battery	

T. Roland Mayler 2nd Lt. R.F.A.
for O/C V/33 H.T.M. B^y.

Army Form C. 2118.

WAR DIARY
or
INTELLIGENCE SUMMARY
(Erase heading not required.)

Instructions regarding War Diaries and Intelligence Summaries are contained in F. S. Regs., Part II. and the Staff Manual respectively. Title Pages will be prepared in manuscript.

31. 5. 17

Place	Date	Hour	Summary of Events and Information	Remarks and references to Appendices
Arras	1.5.17 – 6.5.17		Battery on fatigues at Ammunition Dump and assisting artillery generally.	
"	6.5.17 – 8.5.17		Battery employed on repairing artillery track.	
"	9.5.17 – 18.5.17		Parades each day as follows :– 7.00 a.m. Physical exercises, 10.00 a.m. – 12.00 a.m. gun cleaning and checking stores or route march. 2.00 p.m. – 3.00 p.m. Rifle and box respirator inspection and drill. Guns handed in to Corps Dump.	
"	19.5.17		One N.C.O. and three men for guard over Dump. For remainder of month one man only per day.	
"	20.5.17 – 22.5.17		Parades each day. Physical exercises, route marches and inspections of rifles and revolvers.	
"	23.5.17 – 24.5.17		Battery employed on salvaging unexploded shells at Feuchy.	
"	25.5.17 – 31.5.17		Remainder of battery on following parades daily. 7.00 a.m. Physical exercises. 10.00 a.m – 12.00 a.m	J. Bty recruits with J.H. 16 class at ... for I.C. x 55. J. H. B.

Army Form C. 2118.

WAR DIARY
or
INTELLIGENCE SUMMARY
(Erase heading not required.)

Place	Date	Hour	Summary of Events and Information	Remarks and references to Appendices
ARRAS	1/5/17 to 31/5/17		Battery on Fatigues + Training	

Wingate
O.C. V.33.T.M.B'y.

Army Form C. 2118.

WAR DIARY
~~INTELLIGENCE SUMMARY~~
(Erase heading not required.)

Instructions regarding War Diaries and Intelligence Summaries are contained in F. S. Regs., Part II. and the Staff Manual respectively. Title pages will be prepared in manuscript.

Place	Date	Hour	Summary of Events and Information	Remarks and references to Appendices
	MAY 1917			
	1st to 5th		In billets at ARRAS. Battery engaged in supplying fatigue parties to SPIDER Dump.	
	6th		Reconnoitred trenches in PELVES sector.	
	7th to 14th		Battery in readiness, with two guns, for action in PELVES Sector — bivouac at SPIDER DUMP	
	15th		Returned to billets in ARRAS.	
	16th - 29th		Programme of physical training carried out. Fatigue parties supplied for salvage, dump work etc.	
	30th		Guns of 1/2nd Div brought from railway to mortar park at ARRAS	

E. L. Fitzgerald
Capt
o.c.
Z33 Trench Mortar Battery

WAR DIARY of 1/33 Heavy Trench Mortar Battery
INTELLIGENCE SUMMARY

Sheet 25

33 D T M Bty S
Vol II

Place	Date	Hour	Summary of Events and Information	Remarks and references to Appendices
ARRAS	1st June 1917		Drill pt. 1 N.C.O. and 6 men at Ready Dump	
	2 "		– do –	
	3 "		– do –	
	4 "		– do –	
	5 "		– do –	
	6 "		– do –	– do – 1 N.C.O. & 2 men Rotating party for 29 Div.
	7 "		– do – – 1 N.C.O. and Crew to 156 Brigade R.F.A. Hqs	– do –
	8 "		– do –	– do –
	9 "		– do –	– do –
	10 "		– do –	– do –
	11 "		2/Lt Howell proceeded on leave to England.	– do –
	12 "		– do –	– do –
	13 "		– do –	– do –
	14 "		Captain A. Heads MC RFA – do – rejoined from 3rd Army School of Mortars	
	15 "		– do –	– do –
	16 "		– do –	
	17 "		– do –	
	18 "		Ready Dump party return unit. 156 Brigade R.F.A. party also carrying party for 29th Division return unit.	
	19 "			
	20 "		Moved by lorries from ARRAS to BOIRY St. MARTIN	
	21 "			

WAR DIARY of V/33 HEAVY TRENCH MORTAR BATTERY

Army Form C. 2118.

INTELLIGENCE SUMMARY.

Sheet 26.

Place	Date	Hour	Summary of Events and Information	Remarks and references to Appendices
BOIRY ST MARTIN	22 June 1917		Captain A. HEADS N.C. R.F.A. Accumulated orders to be taken over from V/21 H.T.M.B. at 1 N.C.O. and 15 men laying cable under Adjt instructions.	
	23 "		2/LT. M. HOWELL returned from leave to England	
	24 "		1 gun taken over from V/21 H.T.M.B. – Detachment of 1 N.C.O. and six men. – 1 N.C.O. and 30 men carrying 2" T.M. bombs	
	25 "		Building dug out for detachment and improving gun position	
	26 "		– do –	
	27 "		– do –	
	28 "		– do –	1 N.C.O. & 15 men laying cable under Bge Adjt instructions
	29 "		– do –	1 N.C.O. & 10 men – do –
	30 "		– do –	1 N.C.O. & 15 men – do –
				1 N.C.O. & 15 men – do –

A. Heads.
Major R.F.A.
O/C V/33 H.T.M. Battery

X33 T.M Batt

WAR DIARY
or
INTELLIGENCE SUMMARY
(Erase heading not required.)

Army Form C. 2118.

30-6-17

X33
TRENCH MORTAR
BATTERY.

Place	Date	Hour	Summary of Events and Information	Remarks and references to Appendices
Boyelles	16/17 June 17		Practiced Shoots 7-0 AM Physical Exercise 10-30 AM Rifle and gun school instruction	
	19th		Two R.E. O.R. sent for men prepairing position and mounting of R.E. T.M.	
			Nursery	
	20th		Practice 10 AM Rifle test for Lewis inspection	
	21st		S.O.S positions at 9.30 AM	
Boyelles	22nd		Gun park 10-0 AM. Carried River St. Martin 1-30 PM.	
	23rd		Per R.E.O. one sent on R.E. depot fatigue & mess to two depots etc.	
	24th		Per R.E.O. one Sister men employed on carrying party for ammunition for T33 T.M.B	
	25th		R.E.O. one Sister men R.E. depot fatigue	
	26th		Gun practice 10-0 AM. Final rope for men to use in emergency Gas mask	
	27th		Drill 10 AM Rifle inspection 1-0 PM R.E. depot fatigue all ranks	
	28th		Drill 9 AM 1st battle of Boyelles	
	29th		Rifle inspection 10 AM Box respirator drill 10-30 AM	
Boyelles	30th		Rifle inspection 11-0 AM R.E. depot fatigue 1-0 PM. M.J Blackmore Lt. O. C. X 33 T.M.B	

2449 Wt. W14957/M90 750,000 1/16 J.B.C. & A. Forms/C.2118/12.

WAR DIARY
or
INTELLIGENCE SUMMARY

Army Form C. 2118.

Place	Date	Hour	Summary of Events and Information	Remarks and references to Appendices
ARRAS	1/6/17	11/6/17	Physical Training a guard on Gun Park and Rest Camp.	
-do-	12/6/17	16/6/17	Guards on Gun Park & Rest Camp, Party digging Gun Emplacements for 29th Divn.	
-do-	17/6/17	20/6/17	Physical Training & Guards on Gun Park & Rest Camp.	
	21/6/17		Moved by Lorries to Boiry St Martin	
BOIRY ST MARTIN	22/6/17	30/6/17	Digging Trenches & Carrying Ammunition for Z Battery.	

M Gilchrist M Star
for OC Y/33 TMB

Army Form C. 2118.

WAR DIARY
or
INTELLIGENCE SUMMARY.
(Erase heading not required.)

Instructions regarding War Diaries and Intelligence Summaries are contained in F. S. Regs., Part II. and the Staff Manual respectively. Title pages will be prepared in manuscript.

Place	Date	Hour	Summary of Events and Information	Remarks and references to Appendices
	June 1917			
Cam 3	1" to 5"		Physical training and Battery fatigues	
"	6" " 16"		N.C.O and 10 men assisting 29th Division in making gun emplacements and trench fatigues	
"	17" " 20"		Physical training, Battery fatigues	
Boisy St Martin	21"		Battery moved by motor lorry to Boisy St Martin	
"	22"		O.C Battery took over gun positions from 21st Division	
"	23" " 30"		Battery in action in CROISELLE sector	

J. L. Whitehead
Capt.
OC
233 T M Battery

WAR DIARY of V/33 HEAVY TRENCH MORTAR BATTERY

Army Form C. 2118.

Sheet 2.

Vol 1.

INTELLIGENCE SUMMARY
(Erase heading not required.)

Place	Date 1917	Hour	Summary of Events and Information	Remarks and references to Appendices
BERRY SF MARTIN	1st July		1 Heavy Trench Mortar transferred over to V/33 H.T.M. Battery	
	2 " "		Inspected drill, rifle & previous drill &c	
	3 " "		-do-	
	4 " "		2 N.C.O.s and 18 men fatigue buying parts	
	5 " "		-do-	
	6 " "		-do-	
	7 " "		-do-	
	8 " "		-do-	
	9 " "		-do-	
	10 " "		-do-	
	11 " "		-do-	
	12 " "		1 Officer (2/Lt J.A.Howell R.F.A.) and 11 men proceeded to Belgium - attached to 1st Division Trench Mortars for fatigue purposes	
	13 " "		Inspected drill &c	
	14 " "		-do- 1 N.C.O. and 4 men proceeded to Belgium to join 112 Brigade R.F.A. for fatigue purposes	
	15 " "		1 N.C.O. and 19 men attached to 33rd D.A.C.	
	16 " "		Inspected drill &c	
	17 " "		-do-	
	18 " "		-do-	
	19 " "		-do-	
	20 " "		-do-	
	21 " "		-do-	
	22 " "		33rd Divisional Artillery sports	
	23 " "		Moved by lorries to DOULLENS. (arrived at 1 p.m.)	
	24 " "		Moved by train from DOULLENS to DUNKIRK and thence by lorries to COXYDE BAINS (arrived at 12.30 a.m.)	
	25 " "		Reconnoitred & cleaned rifles &c	

WAR DIARY of 1/V/33 Heavy Trench Mortar Battery. Army Form C. 2118.

or

INTELLIGENCE SUMMARY.

(Erase heading not required.)

Sheet N°

Places	Date	Hour	Summary of Events and Information	Remarks and references to Appendices
COXYDE BAINS	26 Oct 1917		1 N.C.O and 10 men to pumping party for 49th Division	
	27 "		1 N.C.O and 25 men to working party for 66th Division – 1 N.C.O & 9 men returned from 33rd D.A.C.	
	28 "		1 N.C.O and 20 men – do – – do – – 1 N.C.O & 9 men returned from 1st Division	
	29 "		1 N.C.O and 7 men – do – – do – for 9" hows	
	30 "		2 N.C.O's and 26 men – do – – do – – 1 N.C.O & 4 men returned from N° 2 Brigade R.F.A.	
	31 "		1 N.C.O and 5 men – do – – do – for 9" hows	

A Ross. Capt R.F.A.
O/C 1/V/33 H.T.M Battery

Army Form C. 2118.

WAR DIARY
or
INTELLIGENCE SUMMARY
(Erase heading not required.)

31st July 1917

Instructions regarding War Diaries and Intelligence Summaries are contained in F. S. Regs., Part II. and the Staff Manual respectively. Title Pages will be prepared in manuscript.

Place	Date July	Hour	Summary of Events and Information	Remarks and references to Appendices
Berry au Bac	1		Church Parade. Reinforcement 1 O.R. from 33rd R.F.C.	
"	2		Parade. Fatigue party digging trench & burying cable. 2/Lt TH Holmes RFA x/33 TMB posted to Battery	
"	3/4		Divine Service	
"	5		Parade. Fatigue party digging trench & burying cable	
"	6/12		Fatigue party digging trench & burying cable	
"	13		Special Training commenced. Rifle Drill. Instruction on Ammunition. Rifle Exercises. Box Respirator Drill. 1 Offr & 4 O.R. left for 1st div at Cuyse Baine & attached to 1st Div TMB to assist in construction of emplacements	
"	14		Special training continued	
"	15		do	
"	16		Parade. 5 O.R. left for 1st div at Cuyse Baine and attached to 156 Bde Advance Party	
"	17		Parade. 2 O.R. detached to 33rd N.A.C.	
"	18		Parade.	
"	19/21		Parade. 3 O.R. detached to 156 Bde	
"	22		Parade.	
"	23		Parade.	
Doullens	24		G.H. march Artillery Sports.	
"	25		Parade.	
"	26		Regt Rcy St Martin 9am and arrived Doullens at 12 noon (by motor lorry) Parade at Doullens Station 10.30am to load stores. Entrained at Doullens 2.30am. Arrived DUNKIRK 10.30am. Regt disembark'd by motor lorry at 6pm and arrived CUYPE LES BAINS at 6.30pm	
Coxyde les Bains	27		Fatigue Party assisting with Bur. TMS 1 O.R. wounded	
"	28		do	
"	29		do 5 O.R. from 156 Bde returned also R.O.R. from 33rd D.A.C.	
"	30		do	
"	31		do 3 O.R. from 156 Bde returned	

WJ Fieldwick Lt & Adjt
O.C. X/33 T.M.B.

Army Form C. 2118.

WAR DIARY
or
INTELLIGENCE SUMMARY

(Erase heading not required.)

Place	Date	Hour	Summary of Events and Information	Remarks and references to Appendices
BOIRY ST MARTIN	1/7/17 to 22/7/17		Digging Cable Trenches – Physical Training	
	23/7/17		Moved by Lorries to Doullens	
	25/7/17		Entrained at Doullens for COXYDE	
	24/7/17 to 31/7/17		Fatigues & Physical Training	

L Wingate
Lt R.F.A.
O/C Y 33 T.M.B

WAR DIARY
or
INTELLIGENCE SUMMARY.

(Erase heading not required.)

Army Form C. 2118.

Instructions regarding War Diaries and Intelligence Summaries are contained in F. S. Regs., Part II. and the Staff Manual respectively. Title pages will be prepared in manuscript.

Place	Date	Hour	Summary of Events and Information	Remarks and references to Appendices
Bernaville	July 1914		Assisting R.E. making cable trench	
	12 & 13		Guns overhauled & stores overhauled	
	14		1 N.C.O. & 7 gunners part of an advance party sent by 66 Div 4th Bde & 156 Bde Dun making gun emplacements	
	15		5 gunners temporarily attached to 33 D.A.C.	
	16 to 21		Physical training & gun drill	
	22		Personnel Billeted Shoots	
Doullens	23 & 24		Battery move to Fortry and take up billets in Doullens	
Corbie(?) Belgium	25		Battery entrain at Doullens for Corbie	
	26 to 31		Battery fatigues etc. awaiting ammunition to march for 66 Divn 17th Bde —	

L.C. Stevenson
Capt
OC
Z 33 Armd Motor Battery

Army Form C. 2118.

WAR DIARY of /33 Heavy Trench Mortar Battery

INTELLIGENCE SUMMARY.

(Erase heading not required.)

Sheet No. 29.

Instructions regarding War Diaries and Intelligence Summaries are contained in F. S. Regs., Part II. and the Staff Manual respectively. Title pages will be prepared in manuscript.

Place	Date	Hour	Summary of Events and Information	Remarks and references to Appendices
COXYDE BAINS	1917 August 2		1 N.C.O and 3 men to working party for 66th Division (48 hours)	
	" 3		1 N.C.O and 2 men -do-	
	" 4		Gun detail inspection and shell with Respirators	
	" 5		1 N.C.O and 10 men for working party for 66th Division	
	" 6		Rifle drill, Gas Respirators &c	
	" 7		-do-	
	" 8		-do-	
	" 9		-do-	
	" 10		1 N.C.O and 12 men to working party for 66th Division (36 hours)	
	" 11		Rifle drill &c	
	" 12		-do-	
	" 13		1 N.C.O and 12 men to working party for 66th Division (48 hours)	
	" 14		-do-	
	" 15		1 N.C.O and 12 men -do-	
	" 16		-do-	
	" 17		1 N.C.O and 12 men -do-	
	" 18		-do-	
	" 19		1 N.C.O and 12 men -do-	
	" 20		-do-	
	" 21		1 N.C.O and 12 men -do-	
	" 22		-do-	
	" 23		1 N.C.O and 9 men -do-	

Army Form C. 2118.

WAR DIARY of 1/33 Heavy Trench Mortar Battery
INTELLIGENCE SUMMARY
(Erase heading not required.)

Sheet No. 30

Instructions regarding War Diaries and Intelligence Summaries are contained in F. S. Regs., Part II. and the Staff Manual respectively. Title pages will be prepared in manuscript.

Place	Date	Hour	Summary of Events and Information	Remarks and references to Appendices
COXYDE BAINS	1917 August 25		Gas Respirator drill &c.	
	26		1 N.C.O. and 12 men on working party for 66th Division - (48 hours)	
	27		Kit Inspection &c	
	28		Rifle drill &c	
	29		N.C.O and 12 men returned - 1 N.C.O and 20 men Manning 18/pdr ammunition for 33rd Div Battery	
	30			
	31		Rifle drill and Sanybe helmet inspection Inspection of Gas Rations &c	

[signature]
O.C. 1/33 H.T.M. Battery

Army Form C. 2118.

WAR DIARY
INTELLIGENCE SUMMARY
(Erase heading not required.)

X/33' Trench Mortar Battery

August 1917

Place	Date	Hour	Summary of Events and Information	Remarks and references to Appendices
COXYDE BAINS	1/5		Fatigue Party in line assisting 66th Div T.M.s to make emplacements and carry ammunition	
"	6/7		Parade.	
"	8		Church Parade	
"	9		Parade. I.O.R evacuated sick.	
"	10		Parade	
"	11/19		Fatigue Party in line assisting 66th Div T.M.s to make emplacements and carry ammunition	
"	20		Church Parade and do	
"	21/25		do	
"	26		Church Parade and do	
"	27/28		do	
"	29/31		Parades	

W.J. Gilchrist Lt
OC X/33 Trench Mortar Battery

WAR DIARY
or
INTELLIGENCE SUMMARY

(Erase heading not required.)

Army Form C. 2118.

Place	Date	Hour	Summary of Events and Information	Remarks and references to Appendices
COXYDE BAINS	1/8/17 to 31/8/17		Battery assisting 66th Division making Gun emplacements and carrying Ammunition to Gun Pits	

T. Lancaster Munro
Lieut R.F.A.
O/C Y.33 T.M.B.

Army Form C. 2118.

WAR DIARY
or
INTELLIGENCE SUMMARY.

(Erase heading not required.)

Instructions regarding War Diaries and Intelligence Summaries are contained in F. S. Regs., Part II. and the Staff Manual respectively. Title pages will be prepared in manuscript.

Place	Date	Hour	Summary of Events and Information	Remarks and references to Appendices
CLYDE BAINS	1st August to 31st August		Battery assisting 16th Division Trench Mortars, one hvy trench mortar emplacements and carrying ammunition to gun pits.	

M.J.G. Lehmont Lt
for O.C. 2/33 Trench Mortar Battery

Army Form C. 2118.

WAR DIARY of V/33 Heavy Trench Mortar Battery
or
INTELLIGENCE SUMMARY.

(Erase heading not required.)

Instructions regarding War Diaries and Intelligence Summaries are contained in F.S. Regs., Part II. and the Staff Manual respectively. Title pages will be prepared in manuscript.

Sheet No. 31.

Place	Date	Hour	Summary of Events and Information	Remarks and references to Appendices
COXYDE BAINS	Apl. 1		General and signalling	
	2		Fatigues (inadequate) no fatigue rc.	
	3		Move by Motor transport to Hardifort, Nord.	
HARDIFORT	4		"	
	5		"	
	6		Move fm Motor transport to HALLEBAST CORNER nr. DICKEBUSCHE.	
	7		1 N.C.O and 10 men - working party for 156 Brigade R.F.A.	
	8		5 men -do-	
	9		29 N.C.O's and men embusing gun positions - Captain A. HEADS, M.C. R.F.A 'c.	
	10			
	11		2 O.R. returned.	
HALLEBAST CORNER.	12		Captain A. HEADS and 19 N.C.O's and men returned.	
	13		20 O.R. remained, all O.R. returned unit.	
	14		1 N.C.O and 10 men, working party for 162 Bde. R.F.A. - 1 N.C.O 95 men, fatigues 33rd Div Arty (24 hours)	
	15		1 N.C.O and 10 men, fatigues 33rd - Div. Arty.	
	16		1 N.C.O and 10 men, working party in 162 Bde. R.F.A. - 1 N.C.O and 5 men, fatigues 33rd Div. Arty. (24 hours)	
	17		1 N.C.O and 5 men, fatigues 33rd Div. Arty. (-do-)	
	18		1 N.C.O and 10 men, fatigues 33rd Div. Arty. (-do-) - 1 N.C.O and 10 men, working party 156 Bde. R.F.A.	
	19		1 N.C.O and 10 men returned from 162 Bde R.F.A. -do-	
	20		1 N.C.O and 10 men, fatigues 33rd Div. Arty. (24 hours) - fatigues 33rd Div Arty (24 hours)	
	21		1 N.C.O and 10 men for 33rd D.A.C. - 2 N.C.O's and 18 men, working party for 156 Brigade R.F.A.	
	22			
	23		Rifle and Gas Respirator inspection.	
	24		Gas Helmets drill rc.	

Army Form C. 2118.

WAR DIARY of 1/33 Heavy Trench Mortar Battery.

INTELLIGENCE SUMMARY.

Sheet N° 32.

(Erase heading not required.)

Instructions regarding War Diaries and Intelligence Summaries are contained in F. S. Regs., Part II. and the Staff Manual respectively. Title pages will be prepared in manuscript.

Place	Date	Hour	Summary of Events and Information	Remarks and references to Appendices
HALLEBAST CORNER.	Mar. 25		Officer and Ranger inspection	
	26		Rifle drill & Box Respirator inspection	
	27		do- and Box Respirator drill.	
	28		1 N.C.O and 6 men returned from 156 Brigade R.F.A.	
			- do -	
	29		4 men	
	30		Remaining men returned from 156 Bde R.F.A. - 1 Officer and 6 O.R. to School of Mortars - 1 N.C.O and 10 men to advanced Ammunition Dump.	

A. Rass. Capt R.F.A.
O/C 1/33 H.T.M Battery

X/33 T.M.B.

WAR DIARY or INTELLIGENCE SUMMARY

Army Form C. 2118.

HEADQUARTERS,
DIVL. ARTILLERY.
No. B.M.
Date: September 1917

Place	Date	Hour	Summary of Events and Information	Remarks and references to Appendices
COXYDE BAINS	1/2		Barracks	
	3		Left at 9.30 A.M. by motor lorry for HARDINFORT arriving there at 2 P.M.	
HARDINFORT	4/5		Barracks	
	6		Left at 8.15 A.M. by motor lorry for HALLEBAST CORNER arriving there at 12.30 P.M.	
HALLEBAST CORNER	7/12		Fatigue Party to line to assist 33rd Bde RFA in construction of gun emplacements.	
	14		Barracks	
	15/19		Fatigue Party to line to assist 33rd Bde RFA in construction of gun emplacements. 1 O.R. wounded	
	20			
	21		Baths Parade	
	22/29		Fatigue Party to line to assist 33rd Bde RFA in construction of gun emplacements & carrying ammunition. 1 O.R. wounded, one remained at duty	
	30		Fatigue Party to 33rd R.A.C.	
			30.9.17	

W.J. Gilchrist Lt 5ER
o/c X/33 Trench Mortar Battery

WAR DIARY
or
INTELLIGENCE SUMMARY

(Erase heading not required.)

Army Form C. 2118.

Y.33rd M Bde

Place	Date	Hour	Summary of Events and Information	Remarks and references to Appendices
COXYDE BAINS.	1/9/17 to 2/9/17		Cleaning Guns and overhauling Stores	
"	3/9/17		Left Coxyde Bains by motor for HARDIFORT.	
	4/9/17	6.30 p.m	of HARDIFORT.	
HARDIFORT	6/9/17		Left by motor for HALLEBAST CORNER.	
HALLEBAST CORNER	6/9/17 to 7/9/17	6.30 p.m 7/9/17	Digging Gun emplacements for 23rd & 33rd Divisions. also replacing Casualties for 33rd Division	

M. Humphreys 2/L'
for OC. Y33 T.M.B.

Army Form C. 2118.

233/T/M/B/M

WAR DIARY
or
INTELLIGENCE SUMMARY.
(Erase heading not required.)

Instructions regarding War Diaries and Intelligence Summaries are contained in F. S. Regs., Part II. and the Staff Manual respectively. Title pages will be prepared in manuscript.

Place	Date	Hour	Summary of Events and Information	Remarks and references to Appendices
	September			
Couple Brios	1 to 2		Gun Cleaning + Physical Drill	
Morrepont	3, 4		Battery moved and took up billets in Morrepont	
Hale Blanton	5		Battery went to Hale Blanton and bivouac	
	6 to 11		Drilling 2.3" Drummond Artillery in making gun emplacements	
	11		13. People & finishing 9" Holland mounted	
	12, 31		Assisting 33" Divisional Artillery in making gun emplacements and temporarily replacing casualties in batteries	

L.A. Littward
Capt
OC
233 T.M. Battery

Army Form C. 2118.

WAR DIARY
or
INTELLIGENCE SUMMARY.

(Erase heading not required.)

11 V/33 Heavy Trench Mortar Battery

Sheet No. 33

Vol 15

Place	Date	Hour	Summary of Events and Information	Remarks and references to Appendices
HALLEBAST CORNER ——— DICKE BUSCH	1917 Oct. 1		6. O.R. attached to 33rd D.A.C. Rifle and Revolver inspection	
	" 2		-do- and Box Respirators	
	" 3		-do-	
	" 4		Syzijenus - Meaning dump re. 1/4 R. Innerskilling Forts to Battery from the Suffolk Regt.	
	" 5		Rifle inspection -1.O.R. -do- -1.O.R. to course of telegraphy	
	" 6		8 O.R. relieve those attached 33rd D.A.C. - 10 O.R. relieve those attached to Ammunition Dumps	
	" 7		Rifle & Revolver inspection re.	
	" 8		Rifle drill & Box Respirator drill	
	" 9		-do-	
	" 10		-do-	
	" 11		-do-	
	" 12		8 O.R. attached to 162 Brigade R.F.A.	
	" 13		-do-	
	" 14		1 Officer and 6 O.R. returned from course at II Army School of Mortars	
	" 15		9 O.R. to II Army School of Mortars on course	
	" 16		Box Respirator inspection & drill	
	" 17		-do-	
	" 18		10 O.R. relieved those at Ammunition Dumps	
	" 19		8 O.R. returned from 162 Brigade R.F.A.	
	" 20		Rifle drill re.	
	" 21		-do-	

WAR DIARY
or
INTELLIGENCE SUMMARY.

of V/33 Heavy Trench Mortar Battery.

Sheet N° 34

Army Form C. 2118.

Place	Date	Hour	Summary of Events and Information	Remarks and references to Appendices
HALLEBAST CORNER (DICKEBUSCH)	1917 Feb 22		Inspection of Equipment, Arms &c.	
	" 23		5 O.R. joined the Brigade R.F.A.	
	" 24		3 O.R. attached 162 Brigade R.F.A. Returned - 1 O.R. wounded - 8 O.R. Minor Shoe attached 33rd D.A.C.	
	" 25		Rifle drill &c - Captain W. Seacole M.C. R.F.A. proceeded on leave to England	
	" 26			
	" 27		10 O.R. Relieved Shoe attached 33rd Div. forward Ammunition Dump	
	" 28		Rifle & Machine Inspection	
	" 29		- do - + O.R. attached 162 Brigade R.F.A.	
	" 30		9 O.R. reports from H Army School of Mortars - 2/Lt R. Livergren Army Battery from II Army School of Mortars	
	" 3		Inspection of Box Respirators, arms &c.	

Maurice 2/Lt
for Major R.F.A.
O/c V/33 H.T.M. Battery

WAR DIARY
INTELLIGENCE SUMMARY
(Erase heading not required.)

Army Form C. 2118.

October 1917

Place	Date	Hour	Summary of Events and Information	Remarks and references to Appendices
HALLEBAST CORNER	1/4		Fatigue Party 6 O.R. with 33rd D.A.C. Instruction in 6" Newton.	
do	6/8		Fatigue Party 5 O.R. with 33rd D.A.C.	
do	5		1 N.C.O. to 2nd Army School of Trench mortar on Instruction.	
do	9		Fatigue Party 5 O.R. with 33rd D.A.C. Instruction in 6" Newton.	
do	10		do — do —	
do	11		do — do —	Reinforcement 1 O.R.
do	12/22		Fatigue Party 4 O.R. with 33rd D.A.C.	
do	23		do — do —	
do	24		2 O.R. with 162 Bde R.F.A.	1 O.R. wounded
do	25/27		do — do —	
do	28		Fatigue Party 3 O.R. with 33rd D.A.C.	
do	29/31		2 O.R. with 162 Bde R.F.A.	

31 Oct 1917

M.J. Gilchrist Lt
O.C. X/33 Trench Mortar Battery

WAR DIARY
or
INTELLIGENCE SUMMARY

Army Form C. 2118.

Place	Date	Hour	Summary of Events and Information	Remarks and references to Appendices
HALLEBAST (CORNER)	1/10/17 3/10/17		Battery known as Fatigues, men attached to D.A.C. & Field Batteries, building gun positions.	

Y Wingate
Lieut RFA
O.C. Y 33 T.M. Bty

Army Form C. 2118.

WAR DIARY
or
INTELLIGENCE SUMMARY.
(Erase heading not required.)

Instructions regarding War Diaries and Intelligence Summaries are contained in F. S. Regs., Part II. and the Staff Manual respectively. Title pages will be prepared in manuscript.

Place	Date	Hour	Summary of Events and Information	Remarks and references to Appendices
Wallate Corner	October 1917 1 to 31st		Assisting 33rd Divisional Artillery, making gun emplacements and temporarily replacing casualties in batteries and D.A.C.	

L.L. Hitchcock
Capt.
O.C.
Z/33 Trench Mortary Battery

Army Form C. 2118.

WAR DIARY of 1/V/33 Heavy Trench Mortar Battery

Sheet No. 35. INTELLIGENCE SUMMARY.

(Erase heading not required.)

Place	Date	Hour	Summary of Events and Information	Remarks and references to Appendices
HALLEBAST CORNER	1/11/17		17 O.R. to 18 bn. positions forward Battery	
	2			
	3		6 O.R. to Second Anzac School of Mortars	
	4		Move by motor lorries to LE NIEPPE	
	12		Move by motor lorries to BOUVELINGHEM	
	5th Nov – 30 Nov		General Rest – Re-drilling and sports	

Monneau /Major RFA
O.C. 1/33 H.T.M. Bty.

Army Form C. 2118.

WAR DIARY
or
INTELLIGENCE SUMMARY

(Erase heading not required.)

November 1917

Instructions regarding War Diaries and Intelligence Summaries are contained in F.S. Regs., Part II. and the Staff Manual respectively. Title Pages will be prepared in manuscript.

Place	Date	Hour	Summary of Events and Information	Remarks and references to Appendices
HILLEBAST CORNER	1		3 O.R. and 30th Bde. R.F.C. 2 O.R. with 162 Bde R.F.A.	
— do —	2/3		3 O.R. with 33rd Bde. 9 O.R. with 162 Bde R.F.A.	
— do —	4		Moved by Motor Lorries to Le Nieppe. Left at 9 A.M. and arrived at 12.30 P.M.	
LE NIEPPE	5/11		Training comprising 2" Gun Drill, Laying and Ammunition.	
— do —	12		Moved by Motor Lorries to ROUVELINGHEM. Left at 9.45 A.M. and arrived at 1 P.M.	
ROUVELINGHEM	13/30		Training comprising 2" Gun Drill, Laying + Ammunition. 6" Newton Gun Drills, Laying and Ammunition. Route marches. Rifle drill musketry. Bombing.	
				M.J. Gilchrist Lt. 5th S.R.
				O.C. X/33 Trench Mortar Battery
			30th November 1917	

WAR DIARY
or
INTELLIGENCE SUMMARY

Army Form C. 2118.

Place	Date	Hour	Summary of Events and Information	Remarks and references to Appendices
HALLEBAST CORNER	1/11/17		Fatigues & men in action with Field Batteries	
	3/11/17		Left HALLEBAST CORNER for NIEPPE	
	3/11/17 to 12/11/17		Battery training	
	12/11/17		Left LE NIEPPE for BOUVELINGHEM	
	13/11/17 to 30/11/17		Battery training	

Whipple
Lt RFA
O.C. Y 33 TMBty

Army Form C. 2118.

WAR DIARY
of
INTELLIGENCE SUMMARY.
(Erase heading not required.)

Place	Date	Hour	Summary of Events and Information	Remarks and references to Appendices
	November 1919			
Hallast corner	1st to 3rd		Assisting 33rd Divisional Artillery removing guns out of action	
Le Kippe	4th	11"	Battery move by motor lorry to Le Kipper, programme of training carried out	
Bruxellinghem	12th	30"	Battery move by lorry to Bruxellinghem, and continued programme of training	

Hassell Major RFA
O.C.
Z/33 Trench Mortar Battery

Army Form C. 2118.

WAR DIARY
or
INTELLIGENCE SUMMARY.
(Erase heading not required.)

31-12-17.

Instructions regarding War Diaries and Intelligence Summaries are contained in F. S. Regs., Part II. and the Staff Manual respectively. Title pages will be prepared in manuscript.

Place	Date	Hour	Summary of Events and Information	Remarks and references to Appendices
Bouzincourt	1/7.		Training.	
"	2		Left Bouzincourt & met Lewis at 12 mm arrived Harfleur at 4 pm.	
Harfleur	3		Left at 9 AM & met Lewis arrived Warterlinghe at 12-30 pm	
Watterlinghe	4		Moved to Peijpe.	
Peijpe	5		Making camp. 1 OR. evacuated sick.	
"	6		Fatigue parties. 6 Lewis as follows 33rd Div. R.H.	
"	7		" " " "	
"	8			
"	9-13			
"	14		Holiday.	
"	15		2 O.R. evacuated by shrapnel.	
"	16-24		Fatigue parties & Lewis	
"	25		1 Officer & 6 Senior of Motars 1st Army.	
"	26-31		5 O.R. & School of Motors 2nd Army.	
			Fatigue parties & Lewis R.H.A. 33rd Div.	

W. H. Holmes
O.C. 1/4 R.F.A.
TRENCH MORTAR BATTERY.

Army Form C. 2118.

Original

WAR DIARY
or
INTELLIGENCE SUMMARY.

of V/33 Heavy Trench Mortar Battery 33rd R.F.A.

(Erase heading not required.)

Instructions regarding War Diaries and Intelligence Summaries are contained in F. S. Regs., Part II. and the Staff Manual respectively. Title pages will be prepared in manuscript.

Place	Date	Hour	Summary of Events and Information	Remarks and references to Appendices
BOUVELINGHEM	1/7/17			
	2/7/17 3/7/17		Move by march to HARDIFORT – CASSEL. —do— to VLAMERTINGHE	
	4/7/17		Move to advanced public at POTIJZE.	
	5/7/17 – 31/7/17		Holding parties for R.E's. Mounting gun position, dug outs &c	Returns at R.F.A. for V/33 H.T.M. Bty. to V/33 H.T.M. Bty.

33 D TM Bty

Vol 17

WAR DIARY
or
INTELLIGENCE SUMMARY.

Army Form C. 2118.

(Erase heading not required.)

Place	Date	Hour	Summary of Events and Information	Remarks and references to Appendices
	December 1917			
Bouzincourt	1st		Battery completed Programme of Training	
Hardifort	2nd		Battery move by Lorry to Hardifort and take up Billets	
Hamerlinghe	3rd		Battery move by Lorry to Hamerlinghe and Billets in Huts	
Poliyge	4th		Battery engaged in making a camp at Poliyge	
"	5th - 31st		Battery supplies fatigue parties to 33" Divisional Artillery	

Maurice Hepper
fr. O.C. 3/33 Trench Mortar
Battery

SECRET   4/1

C ¥ Q.M.G.

    War Diary (original) for
January herewith.

                        E.C Patrickson
                            Lieut R.E
8/2/14   for   Major R.E
                        O.C 132nd Field Coy R.E

11

33 DTM Btys
January 1918 Vol 18

WAR DIARY
or
INTELLIGENCE SUMMARY
(Erase heading not required.)

Army Form C. 2118.

Instructions regarding War Diaries and Intelligence Summaries are contained in F. S. Regs., Part II. and the Staff Manual respectively. Title Pages will be prepared in manuscript.

Place	Date	Hour	Summary of Events and Information	Remarks and references to Appendices
POTIJZE	1/2		Fatigue Parties to RFA Batteries	
— do —	4		— do — 1 OR wounded	
— do —	5/7		— do —	
— do —	8		— do — 2/Lr T.H. Holmes posted to Z/33 T.M.B	
— do —	9/10		— do —	
— do —	11/20		Making & Repairing shelters in camp	
— do —	21/27		Fatigue Parties to RFA Batteries	
— do —	28		Moved to VLAMERTINGHE	
VLAMERTINGHE	29		Left at 9.15 AM & moved by motor lorries to OUVE WIRQUIN arriving at 4.15 PM	
OUVE WIRQUIN	30/31		Parades	

31 January 1918

M J Gledhall Lt
X/33 Trench Mortar Battery

Y.33 TRENCH MORTAR BATTERY.

Army Form C. 2118.

WAR DIARY
or
INTELLIGENCE SUMMARY.

(Erase heading not required.)

JANUARY 1918

Place	Date	Hour	Summary of Events and Information	Remarks and references to Appendices
VAUX-EN-AMIENOIS	1/1/18 / 5/1/18		Course of Instruction at 4th Army School of Mortars.	
POIZE	6/1/18 / 29/1/18		Attached to Field Batteries for training & Inspection of stores etc.	
OUVE-WIRQUIN	30/1/18 / 31/1/18			

M. Wright
Lieut RFA
O.C. Y33 T.M. Battery

WAR DIARY X/33 Trench Mortar Battery = 33rd R.A.
of INTELLIGENCE SUMMARY. (for information)

Army Form C. 2118.

Sheet 1

Vol 19

Place	Date	Hour	Summary of Events and Information	Remarks and references to Appendices
OUVE-WIEQUIN	30/1/18 to 21/9/18		Announced Robt. Currey this period the Battery was re-organized on the new footing of a 6" Newton Battery under the authority of A.C. 2440 (c) 24/6/18. Capt T. Robertson MAYLER R.F.A. assumed command — the personnel of X/33 R.T.M Batty were transferred over.	
POTIJZE	22/9/18		Joined by Motor Lorries 6 (0) 1 J2E - 606 over the kettles of the 50th Divn. T.M. Batteries. Two positions for mortars under construction were taken over (other 28 N.E.1 D 17 # 4.6.)	
	22/9/18 to 28/9/18		Work continued on these emplacements with assistance from 2/2 Lath C. R.E.	

T. Roosevelt Mayler
Capt R.F.A.

Army Form C. 2118.

WAR DIARY
or
INTELLIGENCE SUMMARY.

(Erase heading not required.)

Y 33 T.M. Battery

Instructions regarding War Diaries and Intelligence Summaries are contained in F. S. Regs., Part II. and the Staff Manual respectively. Title pages will be prepared in manuscript.

Place	Date	Hour	Summary of Events and Information	Remarks and references to Appendices
OUVE-WIRQUIN	1/2/18 – 2/2/18		Training & inspection (Brit: rest) Battery reorganised under new establishment	
"	3/2/18		Left OUVE-WIRQUIN for VAUX-EN-AMIENOIS to attend 4th Army T.M. School	
VAUX-EN-AMIENOIS	4/2/18 – 18/2/18		Course of Instruction	
"	19/2/18		Left T.M. School & returned to POTIJZE	
POTIJZE	23.2.18		Arrived at POTIJZE	
"	25.2.18		Began work on defensive positions in the line at Platt 28 NE1 I.17.a.45.25	

W Winfield Capt. R.F.A
O.C. Y.33 T.M. Bty

Army Form C. 2118.
X/33 Trench Mortar Batty. 33¾ RA
(new formation)

Sheet No. 2.

WAR DIARY
or
INTELLIGENCE SUMMARY
(Erase heading not required.)

Place	Date	Hour	Summary of Events and Information	Remarks and references to Appendices
POTIJZE	1/3/18 to 22/3/18		Construction of the two emplacements for 6" Trench Mortars at (sheet 28. N.E.1. D.17.a.4.6.) continued, with assistance from 212 Field Coy. R.E.	
	23/3/18		Emplacements completed and the two mortars mounted in position.	
	do.		Registered on enemy's defence positions.	
	24/3/18		Constructing Dugout at gun position with assistance from 212 Field C.R.E.	
	30/3/18			
	3/3/18		Abovementioned two 6" Trench Mortars at sheet 28 NE.I D.17.a.4.4. handed over to Y/33 T.M. Battery.	
	31/3/18		Two 6" Trench Mortars emplaced at B.27.c.33.58 and B.22.d.77 respectively D.22.d.80.05 & D.22.d.80.10 taken over from Y/49 T.M. Battery	

T. Howard Myles Captain
o/c X/33 Trench Mortar Battery

33rd Divisional Artillery.

X & Y TRENCH MORTAR BATTERIES

33rd DIVISION :: APRIL 1918

Original
Army Form C. 2118.

X/33 Trench Mortar Battery, 33rd R.A.

Vol 21

WAR DIARY
of
INTELLIGENCE SUMMARY
(Erase heading not required.)

Sheet No 3

Instructions regarding War Diaries and Intelligence Summaries are contained in F. S. Regs., Part II. and the Staff Manual respectively. Title pages will be prepared in manuscript.

Place	Date	Hour	Summary of Events and Information	Remarks and references to Appendices
POTIJZE	1/4/18		Battery in action with TWO mortars, at emplt D24 C.33.5E. emplacement D24 c.33.5E. at D.22. 80.05.	
	10/4/18		Two 6" T. Mortars complete handed to 37th Division.	
	5/4/18		Received 4 – 6"T. Mortars from Gun Park.	
	9/4/18		The two mortars emplaced at abovementioned position dismounted and brought to POTIJZE.	
	12/4/18		Moved by L.S. Wagons to Ypres Barracks. Supplied fatigue parties for 39th Divn.	
	13/4/18		Moved by Ltd. M.Lorries to VLAMERTINGHE. Supplied fatigue parties for 39th Divn.	
YPRES			Awaiting removal orders.	
VLAMERTINGHE	14/4/18			
	15/4/18			
	16/4/18			
	17/4/18		Moved by G.S. Wagons to Browne Camp, Brandhoek Rd. (mapref. A.22 D.85)	
	18/4/18		Supplied fatigue parties for 39th Divn.	
BROWNE CAMP	19/4/18		Three 6"T. Mortars complete handed to 39th Divn and balance of mortars handed over to R.T.O. for return to Base.	
			(6)	
	20/4/18		3 Dismounting removal orders. Supplied fatigue parties for 39th Divn.	
	27/4/18		Moved by L.S. Wagons to QUINTIN. 3 N.C.O's and 20 men attached D.A.C. No 1 Section, 33rd Divn	
	28/4/18		Moved by L.S. Lorries to near Nine Elms Camp. (Mapref. Sheet 27. L.10.C.3.2.) and bivouac there.	
QUINTIN	29/4/18		2 N.C.O's and 10 men attached No. 2 Section, 33rd D.A.C.	
NEAR NINE ELMS CAMP	30/4/18		N.C.O's and men attached D.A.C. 33rd Divn	

T. Ronald Murples
Captain R.F.A.
o/c X/33 T.M. Bty

Army Form C. 2118.

WAR DIARY
or
INTELLIGENCE SUMMARY.
(Erase heading not required.)

Y 33 T.M. Battery

Place	Date	Hour	Summary of Events and Information	Remarks and references to Appendices
POTIJZE (YPRES)	11/1/18 to 12/4/18		4 Guns in action at D.17.c.S.8. Sheet 28.	
	12.4.18		Withdrew guns to VLAMERTINGHE	
VLAMERTINGHE	13.4.18		Supplied Salvage party for 29 Division	
	14.4.18		—do—	
	16.4.18		Left VLAMERTINGHE for BROWN CAMP. A.23.c.2.3. Sheet 28.	
	17.4.18	R7½ yds	Parades & Salvage Parties	
	21.4.18		Returned unsfair to Ordnance Gun Parts	
	28/4/18		Left BROWN CAMP for POPERINGHE. Sent 23 O.R.s to "A" 2 Section D.A.C.	
	29/4/18		Left POPERINGHE for Zouave Camp. L.10.c.2.3. Sheet 27. Sent 11 O.R.s to the 2 Section D.A.C.	

H Wingate
Capt RFA
O.C. Y33 T.M Battery

Original

Vol 22

WAR DIARY of X/33 Trench Mortar Battery, R.A.
INTELLIGENCE SUMMARY.

Army Form C. 2118.

Place	Date	Hour	Summary of Events and Information	Remarks and references to Appendices
NEAR MIRE ELMS CAMP	1/5/18		23 O.R. attached No 1 Section, 33rd A.A.C. and 12 O.R. attached No 2 Section, 33rd A.A.C.	
SH.24.L.10.C.3.2	6/5/18		12 O.R. rejoined from No 2 Section, A.A.C.	
	4/5/18			
	8/5/18		23 O.R. rejoined from No 1 Section, A.A.C.	
	9/5/18 to 14/5/18		Rifle drill and Gas Respirator drill.	
DROGLANDT	15/5/18		Moved to R.A. Dragoons to Drogland Area (Sheet 27 J.11.b.5.4) Gun Drill. Gas Respirator Drill.	
	14/5/18		— do — Lecture by R.A. Divisional Gas Officer on "Gas Discipline".	
	15/5/18		— do — do.	
	16/5/18		— do — do.	
	17/5/18			
	18/5/18		Moved by R.A. Dragoons to Millets in same area (sheet 27 J.b.C.8.4)	
DROGLANDT	19/5/18 to 22/5/18		Programme of training carried out, viz Physical drill, Rifle drill, Gun drill & Gas Respirator Drill, etc.	
	23/5/18		Moved by R.J. Dragoons to Pontypool Camp. (Sheet 27 E.17.f.9.7) and continued programme of training.	
PONTYPOOL CAMP	24/5/18 to 31/5/18		Programme of training continued. 4 O.R. attended course of training on 1 Bn. 2" Lewis at A/162 Brigade daily from 25th May.	

T. Roberts Maylor
Capt. R.F.A.
O.C. X/33 T.M. Battery

Original

WAR DIARY
or
INTELLIGENCE SUMMARY. Y/33 T.M. Battery

Army Form C. 2118.

MAY 1918.

Place	Date	Hour	Summary of Events and Information	Remarks and references to Appendices
Sheet 27 L10 central	1/5/18 to 12/5/18		3rd Off employed with D.A.C. Remainder of battery moved to WINNEZEELE	
	13/5/18			
WINNEZEELE	14/5/18 to 22/5/18		Parades, training etc.	
	23/5/18		Moved to PONTYPOOL CAMP Sheet 27/E 17.d.9.7.	
PONTYPOOL CAMP	24/5/18 to 31/5/18		Parades & training	

[signature]
Lt RFA
for O.C. Y/33 T.M. Battery

Army Form C. 2118.

Sheet 5.

WAR DIARY
or
INTELLIGENCE SUMMARY

(Erase heading not required.)

X/33 Trench Mortar Battery, R.A.

Instructions regarding War Diaries and Intelligence Summaries are contained in F.S. Regs., Part II. and the Staff Manual respectively. Title pages will be prepared in manuscript.

Place	Date	Hour	Summary of Events and Information	Remarks and references to Appendices
PONTYPOOL CAMP 27/E17 G.9.7	1-6-18 to 4-6-18		Programme of training completed.	
	5-6-18		Moved HQ & waggons to 38/A14 a 3.3, and bivouac. 6" Stm Trench Mortars on platform.	
38/A14 a 3.3	6-6-18		Took over 6-6" T.M's emplaced at Posn 1. 38/H23 d 3.3 Gun 2 38/H24 a 10.75 2. 38/H23 d 3.45 Gun 4 38/H24 a 85.30 Gun 6 38/H24 a 20.36 from Y/6 T.M. Battery. Handed 4-6" T.M's complete to 6" Stm Trench Mortars on platform.	
	8-6-18 to 10-6-18		Battery remained in readiness for action.	
	14-6-18		1 N.C.O. on course at Fifth Army School of Mortars.	
	16-6-18		Handed over 6-6" T.M's own to Y/33 T.M. Batty. Took over from them 6-6" T.M's emplaced at 38/H16 c 3.2, 38/H16 c 22.2.2, 38/H9 a 55.10, 38/H9 c 57, 38/H9 d 1.9, 38/H9 a 15.95, in reserve.	
	17-6-18 to 30-6-18		Battery in readiness at these reserve positions.	
	26-6-15 & 30-6-18		Preparing two emplacements for 6" T.M's at H2 C.3.2 and H2 C.3.0 respectively.	
	21-6-18	3 O.R.	sick to hospital with Influenza.	
	22-6-18	4 O.R.	do - do -	
	23-6-18	5 O.R.	do - do -	
	24-6-18		12 O.R. sick with Influenza in isolated bivouac in camp.	
	25-6-18	4 O.R.	temporarily attached for duty from S.A.B.	
	25-6-18	1 O.R.	to hospital with Influenza.	
	27-6-18 & 29-6-18	8 O.R.	returned from hospital, leaving at 30-6-18 5 O.R. in hospital. No sick remaining in camp.	

T. Riverton Murphy
Lieut. O.C. R.F.A. X/133 T.M. Bty.

WAR DIARY
or
INTELLIGENCE SUMMARY.
(Erase heading not required.)

33 DTM By
Vol 23

Place	Date	Hour	Summary of Events and Information	Remarks and references to Appendices
			[illegible handwritten entries]	

Y.33
TRENCH MORTAR
BATTERY.

Army Form C. 2118.

WAR DIARY
of X/33 Trench Mortar Battery 33rd D.A.
INTELLIGENCE SUMMARY.

(Erase heading not required.)

Place	Date	Hour	Summary of Events and Information	Remarks and references to Appendices
28/A.4.a.3.3.	1/7/18		Handed over to Y/33 T.M. Batty. 6-6" T.Ms emplaced at 28/H.16 and 28/H.9 and took over from them 6-6" T.Ms emplaced at 28/H.23 and 28/H.34.	
	7/7/18		Constructing 2 emplacements in English Road.	
	12/7/18		1 O.R. wounded	
	13/7/18		Emplacements in English Road completed and 2-6" T.Ms mounted ready for action. Reported on S.O.S. lines.	
	14/7/18		50 rounds per mortar fired from 2-6" T.Ms in English Road, in support of 6th Bde attack.	
	16/7/18		Handed over three T.Ms to Y/33 Batty, and took over from them T.Ms in reserve at VLAMERTINGHE and BRANDHOEK	
	17/7/18 to 20/7/18		Completing 2 emplacements at H2.C.3.2, H2.C.3.10, and two at G.18.d.	
	25/7/18		Handed over to Y/33 Batty, T.Ms and positions in reserve at VLAMERTINGHE and BRANDHOEK and took over from them T.Ms and positions at 28/H.23 and 28/H.34, and 2-6" T.Ms in English Road.	
	28/7/18 2/7/18		Constructing 2-6" T.M. emplacements in Scottish Wood, and 2-6" T.M. emplacements in Middlesex Road.	

Alister Maugher
Capt. R.F.A.
o/c X/33 T.M. Battery.

Army Form C. 2118.

Y/33 TRENCH MORTAR BATTERY.

WAR DIARY
or
INTELLIGENCE SUMMARY.
(Erase heading not required.)

Instructions regarding War Diaries and Intelligence Summaries are contained in F. S. Regs., Part II. and the Staff Manual respectively. Title pages will be prepared in manuscript.

Place	Date	Hour	Summary of Events and Information	Remarks and references to Appendices
	1-7-17		Handed over to X/33 T.M. Battery 3-in T.M's emplaced at 25/V.23 & 28/V.24 and took over from X/33 T.M.Bty 6-in T.M emplaced at 25/V.16 & 28/V.19.	
	2-7-17		Instructing emplacements at Brandhoek	
	10-7-17		Handed over to X/33 T.M.Battery 3-in T.M's emplaced & Vlamertinghe & took over from them 2 6-in T.M's & English Wood and at	
	17-7-17		Brandhoek	
			Enemy 28/V.23 & 25/V.24	
	12-7		Two personel good registerin on S.I.S. line.	
	17-7-17 6.30 5.5		Improving emplacements	
	18-7		Handed over to X/33 T.M.Btty and took over position in reserve at	
			Vlamertinghe & Brandhoek	
	29/7/5 3/3		Improving emplacements	

J. H. Edwards
Lt. RFA
OC O.B Y/33 TMB

Original

WAR DIARY of X/33 Trench Mortar Battery

INTELLIGENCE SUMMARY

Army Form C. 2118.

Vol 25

Sheet 1.

Place	Date	Hour	Summary of Events and Information	Remarks and references to Appendices
28/M14.a.3.	1/8/18		Battery remained in readiness for action at DAWSON, ENGLISH WOOD and SCOTTISH WOOD positions. Continued construction of 2 positions in Middlesex Wood.	
	2/8/18			
	3/8/18		Handed over these T.M. and positions to Y/33 Battery and took over from them T.M.s in reserve at VLAMERTINGHE and BRANDHOEK.	
	12/8/18		Took over from Y/33 Battery T.M.s and positions at DAWSON, ENGLISH WOOD, SCOTTISH WOOD, and MIDDLESEX WOOD in addition to reserve positions at VLAMERTINGHE and BRANDHOEK.	
	12/8/18 ⑹			
	17/8/18		Battery in readiness for action.	
	18/8/18			
	19/8/18 ⑹		Handed over all T.M.s and positions to Y/33 Battery.	
	23/8/18			
	24/8/18 ⑹		Took over T.M.s and positions from Y/33 Battery. Constructing 2 – 6" T.M. Emplacements at Artillery Camp 41, near KRUISSTRAAT.	
	26/8/18			
	27/8/18 ⑹		All mortars, Beds and Saddles taken out of position brought to B.A.C. Hoyo.	
	28/8/18			
	30/8/18		Moved by Motor Lorry to 27/E.10.a.6.4.	
	31/8/18		Moved by Motor Lorry to PROVEN to entrain next morning for G.H.Q. 3rd Army Reserve Area.	

T. Russell Moyle
Captain R.F.A.
O/c X/33 Trench Mortar Batty

Original

WAR DIARY 1/33 Trench Mortar Battery Army Form C. 2118.

or

INTELLIGENCE SUMMARY.

(Erase heading not required.)

Place	Date	Hour	Summary of Events and Information	Remarks and references to Appendices
27/11/4 C.3	1/8/18		Improving emplacements in reserve positions at VLAMERTINGHE and BRANDHOEK	
	2/8/18		Handed over Trench positions to X/33 Battery and took over from them the T.M. and positions at DAWSON, ENGLISH and SCOTTISH WOODS.	
	to 12/8/18		Handed over to X/33 Battery T.M. positions at DAWSON, ENGLISH and SCOTTISH WOODS in addition to reserve positions at VLAMERTINGHE and BRANDHOEK	
	13/8 to 22/8/18		Took over all T.M.s and positions from X/33 Battery. Battery in action.	
	23/8/18		Handed over T.M. and positions to X/33 Battery. All mortar beds had a set 150 lbs bags put of ncover	
	28/8/18		besides at VLAMERTINGHE and BRANDHOEK. Moved by motor lorry to 27/B.10.b.64	
	30/8/18		Moved by motor lorry to Hedauke to entrain next morning for	
	31/8/18		G.H.Q. 3rd Army Reserve Area	

Sheet 1.
Original

WAR DIARY
of X/33 Trench Mortar Battery, 33rd R.F.A.
INTELLIGENCE SUMMARY
Army Form C. 2118.

(Erase heading not required.)

Place	Date	Hour	Summary of Events and Information	Remarks and references to Appendices
PROVEN	1/9/18		Entrained at PROVEN for Third Army G.H.Q. Reserve Area. Billeted at CANETTEMONT.	
CANETTEMONT	2/9/18 to 13/9/18		Programme of training carried out viz:- Physical Drill, Close order Drill, Gun Drill, Revolver practice etc., including an 11½" participation in Divisional Reserve.	
	14/9/18		Moved by Motor Lorries to LE TRANSLOY	
	15/9/18		Arrived LE TRANSLOY and bivouac	
LE TRANSLOY	16/9/18		15 O.R. and fatigue party at A.R.P.	
	17/9/18 to 18/9/18		do. do. do.	
	19/9/18		Moved to G.C. Wagon to EQUANCOURT then return from A.R.P.	
	20/9/18		Took over 2 L.T. Mortars from 91st T Mortar Batteries	
Equancourt	21/9/18		and emplaced them at X/30 b-4-5	
	22/9/18		Two O.R. wounded.	
	23/9/18		Two guns in readiness for action.	
	24/9/18			
	25/9/18		Supported attack on Green Line by 100th Infantry Brigade	
	26/9/18		and L.A.S. Access to PEIZIERE.	
	30/9/18			

T. Brooke Mayler
Captain R.F.A.
O.C. X/33 T.M. Battery

Army Form C. 2118.

April
WAR DIARY
or
INTELLIGENCE SUMMARY 4/33 Trench Mortar Btty, R.F.A.

(Erase heading not required.)

Place	Date	Hour	Summary of Events and Information	Remarks and references to Appendices
	1/9/18		Entrained at Hiedelsche for G.H.Q. 3rd Army Reserve	
	2/9/18		Arrived G.H.Q. 3rd Army Reserve. Cantlement.	
	3/9/18 to 12/9/18		In Divisional Training	
	13/9/18 14/9/18		Left Cantlement by motor lorry for Le Translog	
	15/9/18		Arrived Le Translog	
	16/9/18		1 Officer and 16 O.R's on fatigues at 33rd D.A. Ammunition Dump. Grécourt	
	20/9/18		moved by G.S. Wagons to Equancourt	
	24/9/18 25/9/18		6.6" T.M. emplaced at X.13.B.90.150	(2 O.R's Wounded) 1 O.R. " 1 Officer killed)
	26/9/18 29/9/18		Fired 61 rounds in Support of Infantry attack. 1 O.R. Wounded Removing Guns from positions. moved by G.S. Wagons to Riencourt	

W. Hapke
Capt. R.F.A
O.C. Y/33 T.M. Bty

Army Form C. 2118.

WAR DIARY
of
INTELLIGENCE SUMMARY
(Erase heading not required.)

X/33 Trench Mortar Battery R.A.

Instructions regarding War Diaries and Intelligence Summaries are contained in F.S. Regs., Part II. and the Staff Manual respectively. Title pages will be prepared in manuscript.

Place	Date	Hour	Summary of Events and Information	Remarks and references to Appendices
PEIZIERE	1/10/18		Emplaced 6 · 6" T.Ms. near HONNECOURT.	
	2/10/18		Patrol party assists R.Es. (with bridge (temporary) over canal de St Quentin near HONNECOURT.	
	5/10/18		Patrol party at Sunfall 33rd Bde. Signals.	
	6/10/18		2 Mobile 6" T.Ms. emplaced in vicinity of AUBENCHEUL-AUX-BOIS	
	7/10/18		Move by G.S. Wagons to AUBENCHEUL-AUX-BOIS	
	8/10/18		Move by G.S. Wagons to MALINCOURT	
AUBENCHEUL	9/10/18		do do do LE FAYT (TROISVILLES)	
MALINCOURT	10/10/18			
LE FAYT.	12/10/18		2 mobile 6" T.Ms. emplaced near MONTAY.	
	13/10/18		As above. 2 mobile 6" T.Ms. emplaced near MONTAY.	
	14/10/18		Fifty rounds fired in support of 38th Div Infantry attack. 2 ORs killed & severely wounded through enemy shellfire	
	15/10/18		2 mobile 6 T.Ms. brought out of line.	
	17/10/18		All 6" mortars taken to A.R.P near TROISVILLES (excepts mobile mortars emplaced near Montay)	
	18/10/18			
	19/10/18		2 mortars (mobile) emplaced near MONTAY fired 60 rounds in support of 38th Div Infantry attack.	
	20/10/18		Patrol party of 19 ORs attacks S.A.A. Station.	
	21/10/18		do do do	
	22/10/18		do do do	
	23/10/18		do do do	
	30/10/18			
FOREST.	31/10/18		Moved to FOREST by G.S Wagons	
	1/11/18		Patrol party return from S.A.A station.	

Remarks and references
No 27
No 26

Raymond Weezersun D.J. Lieut for Capt
o/c X/33 T.M Battery

A5834 Wt. W4973/M687 750,000 8/16 D. D. & L. Ltd. Forms/C.2118/13.

WAR DIARY
or
INTELLIGENCE SUMMARY.
(Erase heading not required.)

Army Form C. 2118.

4/33 Trench Mortar Bty R.F.A.
Oct/18

Place	Date	Hour	Summary of Events and Information	Remarks and references to Appendices
PUZIERE	1/10/18		Fatigue party att 33 Div Arty 33 R.O. signal	
	5/10/18			
	7/10/18		Two Stokes 6" T.M. embussed in rear of m AUBENCHEUL AUX BOIS	
	8/10/18		Moved by G.S. wagons to AUBENCHEUL AUX BOIS	
	9/10/18		Moved by L.S. wagons to MALINCOURT	
AUBENCHEUL	9/10/18			
MALINCOURT	19/10/18		LE.FAYT (TROISVILLES)	
	21/10/18		Two Stokes T.M.s att to 19th Infantry Bde	
	22/10/18		All 6" mortars taken to R.P. near TROISVILLE (except 2 stokes mortar att 19" Infantry Bde)	
	23/10/18		Two Stokes mortar (newtyps) emplaced near MONTAY fired 80 rounds in support of 38 Div infantry attack	
	23/10/18		Fatigue party to 4 R.F.s att S.A.A. Section	
	24/10/18		moved to MONTAY by 4.S. wagons	
	25/10/18		FOREST	
	30/10/18		Two Stokes mortars att 98 Infantry Bde and fired 50 rounds in support of attack	
	31/10/18		Two Stokes mortars att 114 Infantry Bde	

Chas Ritchie 2/Lt. For O.C.

Y/33
TRENCH MORTAR
BTY

WAR DIARY of X/33 Trench Mortar Battery 33rd R.A.
INTELLIGENCE SUMMARY.

Sheet 10.

Army Form C. 2118.

Place	Date	Hour	Summary of Events and Information	Remarks and references to Appendices
FOREST	1/11/18 2/11/18 3/11/18		4 – 6" Trench Mortars emplaced near ENGLEFONTAINE. Fired 150 rounds in holding pts. K.O.R. wounded. Fired 100 rounds in support of 38th Divl. attack, and Battery moved forward in close touch with Infantry with TWO Mobile 6" Trench Mortars until Armistice signed 11/11/18.	
	4/11/18		Hdqrs moved by G.S. Wagons to POIX - DU NORD	
POIX DU NORD	5/11/18 6/11/18		Hdqrs moved by G.S. Wagons to LOCQUIGNOL.	
SART BARA	7/11/18		Hdqrs moved by G.S. Wagons to SART BARA.	
	8/10-11/18		Hdqrs moved by G.S. Wagons to BERLAIMONT.	
BERLAIMONT	11-11-18		At BERLAIMONT. Armistice signed by GERMANY and commenced at 11 hours. Guns brought back to Hdqrs from DIMONT FONTAINE.	
BERLAIMONT	12/13-11-18		At BERLAIMONT.	
CROIX	14-11-18 15-11-18		Moved by G.S. Wagons to CROIX.	
CLARY	16-11-18		Moved by G.S. Wagons to CLARY.	
LES RUES DES VIGNES	17/18-11-18		Moved by MC.S. Wagons LES RUES DES VIGNES.	
	19-11-18 20-11-18 21-11-18 22-11-18		8 O.R's attached 33rd A.G. for duty. 15 O.R's attached 156 Brigade for duty.	
do	23-11-18 to 30-11-18		do do do	

WAR DIARY
or
INTELLIGENCE SUMMARY.
(Erase heading not required.)

1/33 Trench Mortar Bty Army Form C. 2118.
33. R.A.

Place	Date	Hour	Summary of Events and Information	Remarks and references to Appendices
FOREST	1/11/18		6. 6" Trench Mortars employed near ENGLEFONTAINE	
	2/11/18		" "	
	3/11/18		Fired 190 rounds on Loco etc	
	4/11/18		Moved by G.S. wagons to POIX DU NORD.	
POIX DU NORD	5/11/18		" " " LOCQUIGNOL	
	6/11/18		" " " SART BARA	
SART BARA	7/11/18		Moved by G.S. wagons to BERLAIMONT	
	8/11/18		at BERLAIMONT	
BERLAIMONT	14/11/18		Moved by G.S. wagons to CROIX	
CROIX	15/11/18		" " " CLARY	
CLARY	16/11/18		" " " RUES DES VIGNES	
	20/11/18		8 Ors Ott 33 D.A.G. for Duty	
	27/11/18		15 " 162 Brigade for duty	
	to		" "	
	30/11/18		" "	

Y/33
TRENCH MORTAR
Capt RFA
O.C.

WAR DIARY
or
INTELLIGENCE SUMMARY.
(Erase heading not required.)

Army Form C. 2118.

X/33 Trench Mortar Battery R.A.

Sheet No 11

Place	Date	Hour	Summary of Events and Information	Remarks and references to Appendices
Walincourt	1.12.18		Salvaging guns & wagon cleaning. Clearing refuse from streets	Vol 26
Walincourt	7.12.18		Moved by G.S. Wagons to TINCOURT	
TINCOURT	8.12.18		Moved by G.S. Wagons to PROYART	
PROYART	9.12.18		Moved by G.S. Wagons to LONGEAU	
LONGEAU	10.12.18		Moved by G.S. Wagons to DREUIL LES MOLLIENS	
DREUILLES MOLLIENS	11.12.18		Moved by G.S. Wagons to Villers Campsart	
VILLERS CAMPSART	12.12.18		Washing, oiling, greasing wagons	
	13.12.18		10.0.R.s attached to Div Arty	
	15.12.18		Moved by G.S. wagons to INVAL BOIRON	
INVAL BOIRON	16.12.18		10.0.R.s return from Div Arty	
	17.12.18		Cleaning & painting guns. Washing wagons. Sweeping roads.	
do	18.12.18			
	19.12.18		Football match with 6/162 Bde 2nd round Q.A. Competition Result T.Ms 20 C/162 5-3	
	20.12.18		Sunday	
do	21.12.18		Cleaning bullets. Repainting guns.	
	22.12.18			
	23.12.18		X-mas day	
	24.12.18			
	25.12.18		Physical drill. gun drill. Close order drill	
	27.12.18		Cleaning & grand preparation to making gun parts. wagon park etc	
	28.12.18			
	29.12.18			
	30.12.18			
	31.12.18			

[signature]
Capt. R.A.
O/C X/33 T.M. Battery

Army Form C. 2118.

WAR DIARY
of
INTELLIGENCE SUMMARY.

(Erase heading not required.)

X/33 Trench Mortar Btty. H.Q.

Place	Date	Hour	Summary of Events and Information	Remarks and references to Appendices
WALINCOURT	1-12-18 to 6-12-18		Salvaging. Gun & Wagon cleaning, clearing refuse from streets	
	7-12-18		" " " " "	
WALINCOURT	7-12-18		Moved by G.S. Wagon to TINCOURT	
TINCOURT	8-12-18		" " " " PROYART	
PROYART	9-12-18		" " " " LONGEAU	
LONGEAU	10-12-18		" " " " DREUIL-LES-MOLLIENS	
DREUIL-LES-MOLLIENS	11/12/18		" " " " VILLERS CAMPSART	
VILLERS CAMPSART	12-12-18		Washing oiling greasing wagon	
	13-12-18		10 O.R's Left to H.Q 33. D.A	
	14-12-18		Moved by G.S. wagon to INVAL BOIRON	
INVAL BOIRON	15-12-18 to 31-12-18		General Fatigues	

January 1919

Army Form C. 2118.

WAR DIARY
or
INTELLIGENCE SUMMARY.

Y/33 Trench Mortar Battery

(Erase heading not required.)

Instructions regarding War Diaries and Intelligence Summaries are contained in F. S. Regs., Part II. and the Staff Manual respectively. Title pages will be prepared in manuscript.

Place	Date	Hour	Summary of Events and Information	Remarks and references to Appendices
INVAL-BOIRON	12		Captain T. Wingate to England for re-patriation to Argentine M.C.	
	27		Lieut S. Attenborough posted to 162 Brigade R.F.A.	
	29		Lieut H.M. Foulsham & 9 O.R. attached to R.O.C.	
			19 O.R. Unintelligent during the month	

T. Reverend? Mary Lo
Captain
R.F.A.

for O.C. Y/33 T.M. Bty

JANUARY 1919   WAR DIARY X/33 TRENCH MORTAR Army Form C. 2118.
or BATTERY
INTELLIGENCE SUMMARY.

(Erase heading not required.)

Place	Date	Hour	Summary of Events and Information	Remarks and references to Appendices
INVAL-BOIRON	13		LIEUT J.L. KERSHAW. RFA to England for demobilization	
	25		2/LIEUT A SQUIRE SLATER " " "	
	29		13 O.R. attached to D.A.C.	
			18 O.R. demobilized during the month	

T. Kenneth Maples
Captain RFA
Commanding

X.33
TRENCH MORTAR
BATTERY.

WAR DIARY
or
INTELLIGENCE SUMMARY.

(Erase heading not required.)

Army Form C. 2118.

Instructions regarding War Diaries and Intelligence Summaries are contained in F.S. Regs., Part II. and the Staff Manual respectively. Title pages will be prepared in manuscript.

Place	Date	Hour	Summary of Events and Information	Remarks and references to Appendices
Oobigny	January 1st	27th	Battery supply fatigue parties for 33rd Divisional Artillery	
Vlamertinghe	27th		Battery left Oobigny for Vlamertinghe	
Ouve Wippere	29th		Battery left Vlamertinghe for Ouve Wippere by Army	
	30-31st		Battery training	

T. Ronald Maple Capt RFA
O/C
Z/33 Trench Mortar Battery

Army Form C. 2118.

17 33rd T.M. Btys
WAR DIARY
or
INTELLIGENCE SUMMARY.
(Erase heading not required.)

T.M. Batteries:—
X/33. Bty.
Y/33. Bty.

VOL 31

Place	Date	Hour	Summary of Events and Information	Remarks and references to Appendices
NEUVILLE	Feb. 1919		Reduced to Cadre and attached to	
COPPEGUEULE			33rd D.A.C.	
	12/3/19		J.S. Graham Capt	
			Adjutant 33rd Div Arty	

www.ingramcontent.com/pod-product-compliance
Lightning Source LLC
Chambersburg PA
CBHW081544160426
43191CB00011B/1838